ONLY HERE FOR
THE BEER

I wonder if I can sell my forehead for advertising space?

Contents

Introduction
to the original 1978 edition

The death of Gerry Marshall on Thursday 21st April 2005 robbed us of one of the few remaining characters in 21st century motor racing. Public reaction was so overwhelming in the media, and at a funeral attended by literally hundreds, that the author and Haynes Publishing knew this book must be reissued. As prices for original copies had escalated, it seemed appropriate to produce a tribute edition at a more accessible price for what has become an unrepeatable period piece.

Anyone who has an interest in British club-racing will be certain to have heard the name Gerry Marshall, but they may wonder why anyone should write a biography about him? Although Marshall is obviously a good driver, and a lot more versatile than his usual saloon car machinery would suggest, what makes him worth discussing compared with any other saloon car drivers?

I asked myself these questions when I heard that a publisher wanted to do Gerry's life story. Many of the people who raced against Gerry were friends of mine and one in particular – David Brodie – was a respected neighbour, a lot tougher than me, and an arch rival of Marshall's!

I started research for the book in a fairly neutral state of mind, for publisher John Haynes did not produce a veritable empire without employing his enthusiastic and persuasive tongue on the way up. John was, and is, absolutely convinced of the need for this book, a book about one of motor racing's all too rare characters.

By the time I completed my background work I had developed a true respect for Gerald Dallas Royston Marshall. He is an entertaining man in a sport renowned for a high quota of bores.

This witty quality, plus a courageous driving style have endeared him to successive generations of British race-goers. I have written the book for this hardy band of spectators and marshals, the people who have seen him perform in all weathers, for I think Marshall is one of the few who cares enough to make sure the public – the ones who ought to be the most important people in motor racing but rarely are – that the public get a show. Something to cheer for, or even boo. Either way Marshall gives them what they are looking for.

As to the book itself, the content is deliberately not a race-by-race account. I have tried to portray the man within the outsize image. How he lives and some of his motoring adventures. The chronological order suffers – as it does when Gerry himself is talking to you – by the insertion of so many tales. That is Marshall though, a fascinating collection of stories that go to make up a super motoring enthusiast. A man who has had the gumption to go and do so many of the things that most only dream about, but has managed to do so without sacrificing the quality of normal everyday life for Superstar status.

I have devoted considerable space to the role of Vauxhall in Gerry Marshall's racing life. I make no apology for so doing. So far as I am aware nobody has tried to tell the story of how this branch of General Motors restored its self-respect through sporting activities. Since the story of that revival and Marshall's coincide at most points it seemed a worthwhile exercise.

Unfortunately, some people will inevitably be offended by some sections of the book. To those who are, I offer this morsel of cold comfort – you should have seen what we took out!

Jeremy Walton, September 1978

Introduction
to the 2005 Tribute Edition

The day Mr British Motor Racing died

Thursday, 21 April 2005, Silverstone Circuit, Northamptonshire. Gerald 'Gerry' Marshall's ardent appetite for every outing in a racing car – particularly any muscular V8 saloon – had been satisfied with a borrowed 1972 Chevrolet Camaro. It had been a frustrating morning, working the pit lane on a public practice day on the trail of another adrenalin fix. Time now for the next shot of the exhilaration that fed Gerry's voracious hunger for automotive satisfaction. Sadly though, this would be the last one, because he died, behind the wheel. The cause of death was "heart-related illnesses" rather than the simple heart attack of contemporary reports.

The aged General Motors machine "drifted to a halt on the outside of the sweeping Luffield right-hander, a short distance from the British Racing Drivers' Club clubhouse," reported *Motorsport News*. "Although emergency services arrived on the scene within minutes, Marshall never regained consciousness and was pronounced dead at the scene." The British weekly paper drew on eyewitness accounts that poignantly added that this true professional managed to switch the engine off before he died the most appropriate of racing deaths. For Gerry was not only in a racing car but within sight of the BRDC club that was so much a part of the Big Man's legendary capacity for squeezing the most from business and track life at the bar.

The *Motorsport News* tribute ran to over nine pages, yet Grand Prix drivers and similar international stars rate a page or more only if they are larger than life characters in the James Hunt mould. It was not just *Motorsport News* at the grassroots of national automotive sports that went for this kind of major Marshall obituary either. *Autosport* peppered their next issue with over five pages of tributes, including the serious suggestion that Luffield should be renamed Marshall's as a mark of respect.

In the printed media, the obituaries continued to astonish and delight those who had supported Gerry through the adversities of primitive UK circuits in the 1960s and 1970s. For we had faced the grubby realities of British fast food, foul weather and facilities that were downright hostile when Marshall started thrilling motorsport enthusiasts with the biggest broadside slides of all, 41 years before his death at the age of 63.

Even the posh classic/historic car glossies became Marshall tribute bands. When the *Daily Telegraph* ran a half page, it proved finally that Gerry's character and sheer entertainment value had put him among the motor racing Gods, the stars who appeal to a wider public. Indeed he was the king of spectator hearts for the people that should count – but seem to be despised by 21st century Formula One – the paying public.

Initially it looked as if it would be a parochial British affair, this mourning the passing of a hero built for exploits on a larger scale, but when the World Wide Web sites started flickering out the news, the international reaction overwhelmed any expectation – see pages 7–12 for some of the many internet obituaries.

Gerry had a spectacular send-off. Some 550 people attended the funeral, held at 12 noon on Friday, 6 May, at Garston Crematorium, Watford, Herts. It was an honour to be present at this alternately funny and sad celebration of a life that had touched so many others, including three wives and his constant companion in later years. Carol Maynard married Gerry in 1965 and they had three children, but their marriage was annulled in 1981. Gerry's second marriage was to Jennifer Cook. This ended in a divorce, in 1988, although – as Gerry did with all his ex-wives – they remained in touch. He married a third time, to Penny Dealey, although that union also ended in divorce. For most of his last five years Gwen Howard was Gerry's constant companion. She was a consistent source of practical strength through some of his darkest days, fighting the after effects of major heart bypass and surgery to his spine, knees and hip.

Even though I was his biographer I did not learn until the service address by principal speaker John Llewellyn and subsequent comments from Ruby – Gerald's mother – that the 'Royston' part of his name was adopted unofficially. Incidentally, none of the family were sure why Gerry added 'Royston' to his given forenames of Gerald Dallas, but it was typical of the man to leave another enigmatic puzzle behind – one that would have all the journalists getting it wrong! I can almost hear a glass clinking as Mr Marshall grins down at us poor mortals, muttering "even if you knew all my names you'd spell them wrong… dreadful hacks, the lot of you!"

I also learned that Gerry had two younger brothers (John and Martyn). And that he did not plan his own – very appropriate – funeral service. Offspring Tina, Justine and Gregor, plus Gwen, concocted proceedings to deliver the best possible taste of Marshall favourites.

The service was not the end of that memorable day. The Marshall family, including 89-year-old Ruby, had arranged a gathering at the gracious and spacious upstairs ballrooms of Pendley Manor Hotel, which was not far from Gerry's modest home in his final years, at Tring. We toasted Gerry's life at the bar, told increasingly unlikely – but hazily truthful – tales of a mischievously merry life, celebrating Gerry's large impact on the smaller UK club motor racing community.

Historic visage, historic saloons and another action event ahead. *LAT*

Gerry's death drew together many who had not seen each other in 20 years and more, yet conversations from paddocks up and down the land seemed to be resumed seamlessly. I owed the Big Man a thank-you alongside the hundreds of others – some famous, some infamous – all sincere in their desire to commemorate Gerry's extraordinary life.

At one end of the sunny rooms was a reminder of the Big Man hustling around Oulton Park, all arms and elbows, on films from the DTV era. The other side of Gerry's character, as a family man with the latest of his four grandchildren, was portrayed with pictures from his personal album. There were perhaps 30 pictorial records of a private life in which family was definitely the top priority.

Towards the end of his life Gerry suffered ill health but, despite recurrent pain, he kept right on racing whenever the authorities would let him have a competition licence, and his ability to entertain us remained undimmed…

Post-1978 racing: the legend lived on
Gerry Marshall claimed 623 motor racing victories, covering both class and outright success. We unearthed 14 outright British national championships and seven class titles seized by Gerry between 1971 and 1983, a remarkable record in itself. Most fans would expect 90 per cent of that staggering total to have been taken in DTV Vauxhalls (63 wins driving the 'Old Nail' Vauxhall Firenza), or Ford Capris/Escorts or Triumph Dolomites, but the truth was more complex.

The legend would support the big motor, big horsepower, rear-drive cars as Gerry's most effective weapons, but he was a winner with less than 100bhp, defeating subsequent World Champion Jody Scheckter in the 1971 Escort Mexico Challenge. More predictably he also racked up 14 victories via the practically invincible 476 horsepower of the DTV 1975-77 *Baby Bertha* Vauxhall, the charismatic V8 racer Marshall bought and sold, twice.

Yet this flip précis of a saloon car career still does the Big Man no justice. When I talked to Gerry for *Classic & Sports Car* magazine in spring 1999 he recalled winning 100 events in Aston Martins, mostly backed by the totally loyal Geoffrey Marsh. The popular image would be of Gerry in a Marsh Plant Hire-backed DB4, and it was in such an Aston that he took his 600th reported victory during year 2000 at Snetterton. That was some 36 years after his first car race at the same East Anglian track, piloting a Mini.

Gerry's fondest Aston memory was of the Lloyds and Scottish seasons in the Marsh collection Aston Martin DBR4 Grand Prix single-seater. He reported of the 1981 Silverstone Grand Prix supporting event: "The front row featured myself in Geoffrey's Aston, Willie Green in the Ferrari Dino single-seater and Robs Lamplough's P25 BRM."

Gerry explained: "It turned into a wheel-to-wheel fight with Willie, with some nose-to-tail interludes. Even in GP cars you could hear the huge crowd shouting for more. That win was special, and so was Roy Salvadori's comment on our performance, saying that we would not have disgraced ourselves in the Grands Prix of years ago".

Other winning ways, that might have escaped all but the committed Marshall watchers, included winning the 1981 Dubai GP in a Lola T70, the near-domination of the 1991 TVR Tuscan title – some 30 years after he had first thundered to the fore in a 1960s TVR Griffith and original Tuscan – plus a strong affection for Jaguars, open and closed. These including the Listers that he owned and raced for others, the inevitable E-types and some typically classic 3.4- and 3.8-litre saloons. There was also a lot more Ford success than you would expect of the Vauxhall-GM name, including a quartet of outright Production championship wins in a 3-litre Capri, a class series win in the Ford coupé and that second place on the 1974 Avon Tour of Britain with an Escort RS2000.

Gerry also drove other unlikely machinery with varied success, usually on a one-off basis. Here I am thinking about the 1971 Costin Amigo, Ivan Dutton's beautifully detailed Alvis Grey Lady of 2004 Goodwood Revival fame, Alan Foster's Morris Marina and a hapless Hillman Avenger that looked a like a rental car. There were also outings in the SAAB one-make series of 1987 and the 1988 Uniroyal P100 championship. I particularly remember him clambering from a ridiculously small Suzuki at Oulton Park in 1988: the man would drive *anything*, even when it had no overall chance.

An unheralded side to Gerry's racing life was his backing for a diversity of racing talent. How he sponsored World Champion Denis Hulme in an Opel for the 1976 Tour of Britain is recorded in this book, but there were ten other deals he recalled. These included multiple associations with Tony Lanfranchini and Jock Robertson, plus Prime Minster's son Mark Thatcher [Willhire Capri], the effective Barbara Cowell [Fiat/Vauxhall], saloon aces such as Patrick Watts [now in a Sunbeam Tiger rally car] and Karl Jones [Escort Turbo/Abarth 130].

Sadly, *Only Here For The Beer*, published in October 1978, missed many of Gerry's later achievements. But on 9 February 2002 his importance was celebrated by the British Automobile Racing Club who presented him with a gold medal for his "outstanding contribution to British motorsport". BARC chief executive Dennis Carter commented: "There is no doubt that Gerry merits a gold medal, not only for his remarkable total of over 600 race wins, but also for the enjoyment he has given his many followers."

The next four pages give an idea of the enthusiasm of those fans. Then read on, remembering that most of the quotes came straight from contemporary 1977-8 tape recordings, some taken on his morning M1 dash to a day's motor dealing, story telling, spoof and mayhem. Sadly, we will never see another Big Gerry enriching 21st century motorsport…

Jeremy Walton, July 2005

Left: Gerry and his first wife Carol, with his then collection of cars and bikes.
The Marshall Family Archive

Right: Big man bullies small trike at Goodwood Revival, 2001.
LAT

Internet obituaries

Here are some samples of more than 200 posted, including many like the Portuguese posting we reproduce here. This first batch is from www.ten-tenths.com/forum

I first saw Gerry's unique style at Brands when I was a flag marshal in my teenage years and I always made a point of having a quick hello with the man at Goodwood. Seeing Gerry driving the nuts off that Alvis last year was fantastic, he must have been laughing his head off in the car. It was also good to see him out of the buggy and walking a lot better than recent years. A good man and a great racer – RIP. Thank you and regards. **John Norris**

So sad news.
First met Gerry late 1972 when he came to Estoril and entertained the crowd with his both strong and hilarious drive of the DTV Firenza 2300 in the G1 race. Another departure of a remarkable man that leaves us poorer. **Carlos Guerra, Cascais, Portugal**

Hard to believe that I won't be watching the big feller again. I first saw him at Oulton in 1966 when he drove the Barmoco TVR Griffith in the GT race supporting the Gold Cup. I remember he had "SODS" in capital letters on the door pillar, and he never disappointed thereafter. You knew that, if he lined up on the grid, he would give 100%, no matter which class he was in, or whatever the opposition. He has certainly given me more entertainment than any other driver I can think of, for which, thanks.

My abiding memory of him is when he drove Nick Mason's V16 BRM in an unscheduled demonstration at a VSCC April Silverstone meeting about ten years ago, and drove it like I have never seen anyone else demonstrate a V16 BRM before or since – including Jackie Stewart at the 1966 Gold Cup, which was pretty spectacular. Shame we never saw him race it. **Alan Cox**

Above: The original book was launched at Ronnie Scott's Jazz Club in London. Marshall, forced to drink wine, attempts to stop author Jeremy Walton from talking. *Ted Walker/Ferret Fotographics*

Below: Gerry in a hurry with the fabulous Ivan Dutton Alvis, Goodwood, 2004. *LAT*

Above: Gerry performed superbly in this Healey against heavyweight opposition at the 2004 Goodwood Revival race meeting. *LAT*

Motoring book retailer Simon Lewis added on that Silverstone V16 BRM demonstration:
I stood on the inside at Copse in the mist with my late father (always a fan of Gerry) as the car shrieked into sight and we were spellbound as it twitched sideways when a brake grabbed. Anyone else in such a car (valuable, delicate and not exactly known to handle well...) would have at the least lifted off but Gerry stuck his right foot down and was sideways through the corner at about a million revs! I have never heard or seen the V16 so properly used before or since. It was mesmeric. The guy could REALLY drive a racecar. Any racecar! **Simon Lewis**
The following three were posted at: –
www.pistonheads.com/gassing

I remember many races together, 1968 to 1974, both on the track and in the Bar!! One stands out in the early days of Group 5 at Thruxton, me in my road-going Mini, when we swapped tapes on the line (CDs hadn't been invented then). After which Gerry downed the dregs of a pint of beer perched on the roof of his car (later banned by the RAC steward, bad influence), and amused the crowd with strains of 'Hair' (Age of Aquarius) and other music as we negotiated the chicane. Him in front...of course. RIP Gerry. **Tony Pearce**.

Gerry and I shared a Firenza in Thundersaloons in the mid 1980s. At Snetterton we led the class and Gerry had a "robust" tussle with David Lesley's Opel Manta which involved the Firenza getting ahead, and the Manta taking to the grass. Now – the chat in the bar afterwards is something that I really wish I had videoed! John Cleland was there too and everyone (including David) ended up rolling around laughing with the Big Man. What a great bloke! We will all miss ya Gerry! **Tony Davies**

What a sad, sad day. My father-in-law sponsored Gerry in the Shaw and Kilburn Viva in 1970 and my wife, who was a kid at the time, says what a hoot he was to be around – her mother disapproved of Gerry which was always a good sign!

I remember that at some stage in the 1970s they organised a running race along the start/finish straight at Silverstone. All the fit young drivers lined up whilst Gerry rolled out of the bar and whipped them all.

A great character – we're all the poorer for his passing. **Jasper Gilder**

This one is rude, but Gerry often combined wit with Saxon dialect. If you are offended by sexual innuendo, continue to the next tribute, but you'll miss the flavour of the man.

My abiding memory of Gerry Marshall is at Thruxton in 1994. Having raced earlier in a modified Aston Martin, he was discussing Nigel Mansell's imminent (but as yet not formally confirmed) return to Williams from Indycar for one-off races with the Williams mechanics.

"He may be a wanker," said Marshall, "but he's a fast wanker!"

It's made me laugh ever since. **Anon**

Here is a vivid independent account of the Gerry Marshall funeral on a site hosted by Cottage Classics as: – www.gerrymarshall.co.uk.

Despite being an hour or so early for Gerry's funeral we could only secure a standing position in the lobby of the chapel. Hundreds of friends, family and distinguished members of the BRDC packed the chapel, balcony, stairs, lobby and overflowed outside. As we waited outside, the minister arrived in his shiny BMW and we heard him say "Good grief! What are we going to do with all this lot?"

The car park was full, and overflowing down the road for hundreds of yards was an impressive array of Astons, Porsches and Maseratis. The Alvis Grey Lady, raced at Goodwood last year, was in attendance and so was Gerry's own Ford Model A (driven by son Gregor), amongst abundant other classics.

The humanist ceremony was touching, respectful and at times, unsurprisingly, amusing. Assembling to the strains of "My Way" and "The Entertainer" one could only suspect that the event had been plotted by Gerry himself with much merriment in the pub! The coffin was decorated with a winner's garland, a chequered flag, Gerry's old racing helmet, and BRDC stickers.

After a touching and well researched address by [humanist] Simon Allen and a fitting personal tribute by John Llewellyn, our suspicions were further confirmed when Willy

Left: Familiar, but still stirring sight: Gerry drives the Marsh Plant Aston DB4, this time lifting a wheel at Brands Hatch. *Gary Hawkins*

Above: The family man, holding his eldest grandson, Harry Gerald Lynch. This picture was taken at Snetterton in 2000 when Gerry won his 600th race. *The Marshall Family Archive*

Right: One of the best portraits taken of Gerry, especially in his later yars, this Gary Hawkins study of Gerry reunited with Baby Bertha at Brands Hatch was also chosen for the cover of the funeral service schedule. *Gary Hawkins*

Above: Gerry Marshall + BRM = maximum spectacle! *The Marshall Family Archive*

Below: Respect from the Vauxhall VXR race team at Thruxton, 2005. *LAT*

Barrett stood up and "sang" a boisterous song involving a duck and the sea being made of whisky. Somewhere in the back of my mind we had heard of Wild Willy Barrett and suspect that this may indeed be the same chap. His violin technique was certainly not for the faint hearted! The whole memorable affair was drawn to a close by Willy Barrett's unique version of "Wish Me Luck As You Wave Me Goodbye".

Sublime. It was an honour to have been there. **Spadge Hopkins**

The entertainer

For thousands of British motor racing spectators, and a surprising number abroad, Gerry Marshall is not a mere racing driver, he is an institution. His amazing car control on the track is a vital ability, for here is one of the few modern drivers who is unhappy unless he's travelling sideways with the crowd baying for more. Marshall - 'Gerald' to his parents, Gerry to everyone else - is not one of the current technocrats of racing science, who happen to be motor racing because it's the most enjoyable laboratory they can find. No, Marshall, on or off the track, is a much larger than life character of the kind that used to go motor racing years ago. His reason for being out there racing is simple: he enjoys it more than anything else (yes ... even that, or the other!) he does in a hectic life.

Just as the man is much more complex than his bluff King Henry VIII dimensions would suggest, so his activities off the track are equally complicated. A working Marshall day is quite likely to involve every nook and cranny of the rest of the Britain so inconveniently clustered around his home, which is some fourteen Marshall motorway minutes north of his sporting secondhand car showrooms in Finchley Road, North London.

Motor trading is the obvious business life for Gerry. He is extremely sociable, very shrewd and seemingly fearless in the face of overwhelming quantities of alcohol! While the rest of Gerry shakes with mirth and produces yet another tortuous tale, another corner of his mind will record a car's county of origin, any sporting record or scandalous owner, vehicle history and its value. He is still a performance car addict and will drive anything that looks remotely interesting, ancient or modern, on the road or in competition. His motor racing knowledge is similarly encyclopaedic, though even he admits to losing track of the hundreds who take part in Formula Ford single seater racing today.

As you will read, Gerry Marshall was brought up midst a motor racing background, but parental opposition led to some typically hilarious outings in rental fleet Minis before our resourceful hero emerged, ready for an audience already primed for his first racing appearance by his spectacular performance in 'grass roots' motor sport. From the beginning he was always fine value for the cold, wet and often muddy British racing spectators. That brave army of souls in the Dunlop or Les Leston rally jackets of the early sixties took to Gerry in a big way. His handling of a Mini stood out, even amongst the large crowd of young men then apparently committed to mass-suicide in Alec Issigonis' amazing little box. Then came TVR and Lotus sports cars, more Minis and a positive plethora of every conceivable saloon car for racing, rallying, even rallycross and especially sprinting or hillclimbing, his second loves after motor racing proper.

Despite the fleets of cars that big burly Gerry has seemingly never grown tired of testing his sideways style in, one marque has occupied his life for a decade, almost to the exclusion of all others: Vauxhall. So this book sets out to tell you how it was that Marshall and a qualified Dutch-Norwegian aeronautical engineer - W.B. 'Billy' Blydenstein -

became involved. Having joined forces it tells the story, as truly as the laws of the land and reasonable language permit, of the team that grew up in a converted railway station. How a small number of fiendishly hardworking men turned the Luton marque from an interesting competition joke to a dominant force in club racing through the legendary 160mph Firenza V8 Baby Bertha. The book also explores how the unstoppable success of Big Gerry and Baby Bertha eventually tolled the death knell for Dealer Team Vauxhall in racing, leading these Vauxhall representatives to abandon the sport that had re-established the honour of the Vauxhall name. How they dropped a secret project to race an 8.1 litre Can-Am Vauxhall Cavalier, and went into their present fight for rallying supremacy in the British forests against Ford and Fiat, is also recounted.

That cruel but commercially sensible decision left Gerry to fend for himself in motor racing once more, a task he settled to with characteristic vigour in a Triumph Dolomite Sprint and a Ford Capri 3000S. But Marshall still represents Vauxhall's sporting ambitions in many eyes and we follow him through one of the many forums that he still participates in on their behalf, where Gerry's frank talking and superb off-the-cuff humour come through at their best.

When we sat down to discuss the outline for this book, Marshall took one look at the contents and pinpointed the obvious omission in so many motor racing books. He said: "Yes, great, but what about Gerry, the person?" I spluttered excuses while running through our ten year acquaintance, which has spanned periods of verbal war to supporting the same bar. Well, he usually supports it, I'm either underneath by that stage or dancing on top! GM - he swears the company is named after him, rather than a deliberate name change in film starlet manner - anticipated my chief worry neatly. "Don't worry, you can say the bad things as well, but say them pleasantly!" Faced with the 'Glittering Prize' of starvation as an alternative, I quickly acquiesced and agreed to the character assassination - I mean impartial observation of course - though I couldn't decide for the life of me where it should appear in the book. At the end it would sound like a school report, besides which you should have made your own minds up by then. So I think I'll get it over and done with now. Before I do let me just add, for the benefit of those using W.H. Smiths as a public browsing facility, that the book also contains unexpurgated accounts of Gerry's racing career (including the controversies); tall trading stories (how petrol pumps are a negotiable currency); as many excerpts as I have been able to negotiate from his *Cars and Car Conversions, Motor* and *Autosport* columns; an attempt to recount some of the highlights amongst the many cars he has driven, and a rather more serious look at the often low budget, but very effective DTV machinery provided for him, including such characters as *Old Nail, Big Bertha, Baby Bertha,* and his often overlooked production racing mounts.

If my fumbling attempts at character assassination have failed, a host of so-called friends have done their best to finish Gerry's chance of ever power-sliding an Angelic chariot with their own pungent observations. You will meet even more unlikely characters, such as Barry 'Squeaker-Whizzo' Williams, one of Gerry's rather more aristocratic friends, and the inevitable Big Tone, otherwise known as Tony Lanfranchi, the final member of a fearsome motor racing trio that has been known to haunt circuit bars, almost until closing time, whatever the cost to their clean cut features.

Now to unveil the real Marshall beneath a weight that increases in each interview, almost in direct proportion to the loss of years in each successive account! In simple terms Gerry Marshall's emotional make-up is magnified in the same way as his physical appearance. He feels things strongly and seems totally unafraid of expressing his views without diplomatic filtering. If you met him for the first time among a crowd gathered in après motor race meeting honour of his latest outing, there is little doubt that the impression would be that of, at least, a man heartily enjoying himself. The quieter your disposition, the more likely you would be to come away thinking: "What a braggart!"

However, if you are capable of standing while the seas of booze threaten to wash you

John Fitzpatrick, myself and Warwick Banks fight it out at Crystal Palace for the 1-litre class in the British Championship: I was second on this occasion. *Courtesy Evan Selwyn-Smith.*

I was a happy little chap at Lydden Hill in 1965.

away, and contributing the odd quip, the chances are that you would come away think-ing: "– me! A motor racing character, a real man amongst the boys!" In motor rallying, where the influx of talented Finns with their stern drinking habits sets different standards of behaviour, Gerry Marshall would cause little comment. His sideways driving style would seem natural too, but in the often deadly serious world of circuit racing (where it often pays in lap time to be as neat in your driving as possible, especially in an under-powered car of the type Marshall frequently drives) he sticks out not like a sore thumb, rather as a great inflamed foot, stirring vigorously!

It's interesting to note that rallying is often the subject of great longing in Gerry's heart, and there seems little doubt that he would accept any decent chance to try to establish it as his prime competition activity. This, despite the frequent Marshall references that run along the lines: "When I get old and slow I'll go rallying", and, "If you can't find anything better to do on a Saturday night than sit with another sweaty fellow and destroy a perfectly good motor car, then you deserve to be a rally driver!"

As one of Gerry's closest friends says later in the book, Gerry is a very different person away from the bar and a crowd! Aren't we all? Not to quite the same degree. You see Gerry Marshall is also capable of the generosity often found in genuinely 'big men'. He can be extremely generous, his quick temper matched by the kind of thoughtfulness that led to his opting out of motor racing for nearly a season in order that his fiancée should " ... wear a Mini-Cooper on her finger". In other words he sold his racing car to buy the engagement ring. He is a great one for the family side of life, though the constant need to reassure himself through constant racing pulls him apart at weekends, his charm-ing wife Carol and their three children balanced on the scales fairly equally against the attractions of a motor racing weekend. Even though he has a fair claim to being on his dignity as an international driver of some worth, he is equally likely to plump for a Saturday driving a friend's Mini and a Sunday in some apparently antediluvian 'classic saloon' just racing for fun.

Those that would doubt his actual racing ability are on dangerous ground. Marshall's forthright personality and extrovert lifestyle are not sought-after ingredients in international racing teams. The kind of racing he excels in, endurance racing at speed, of the kind found in the Spa-Francorchamps 24 Hour races, relies on team work. Gerry is patently not a team man; he gives of his absolute best all the time - so he needs a pretty strong car under him - and if there are any snags people will hear about it ... all the way down the pit lane! Thus he is unlikely to curry much favour in a team manager's eyes and this has undoubtedly cost him opportunities that his inborn talent could have capitalised on.

In saloon car terms he is better than 97 percent of drivers racing in the world today - and those that are better have generally reaped the rewards in other classes of racing. There are two telling performances of Marshall's when discussing his international aspirations. At Spa he backed up the promise of years by taking a 2300cc Group 1 1/2 Vauxhall Magnum to second overall (splendidly partnered by Peter Brock of Australia, the two well-matched in lap times) against much faster cars on a track that emphasises flat-out speed. The second international outing of significance was in 1974 when Stuart Turner, a man not renowned for sentiment, picked Marshall to drive the second works Ford RS2000 on the Tour of Britain. Now, the lead driver was Roger Clark, who is at least as good as most professional touring car drivers on tarmac and totally superior on the loose. Marshall not only proved a complete professional under strong provocation from Roger he also chased the maestro every inch of the way. Though Turner nicknamed the two generously proportioned drivers 'Écurie Beer Gut', they emerged as convincing out-right winners of the event, Marshall also showing fine acumen in rating Vauxhall's chances on the Tour, as the Luton cars were thrashed in the process, Marshall's mate Lanfranchi bringing a big BMW home third. Throughout this event Gerry stayed calm, and surprised everyone with his loose surface skill. In this and a subsequent Tour he

Boxing Day at Brands 1965, and I enjoyed a good run against John Sparrow's Cobra and a particularly fine dice with David Piper's Ferrari.

Driving with considerable pieces of Elan! I never liked the car much after this. *Courtesy Mike Kettlewell.*

actually beat all the rally aces on a loose stage, something no other racing driver can lay claim to, though many rallyists have beaten the racers on tarmac in this event. To my mind this established his all round skill in the same way Stirling Moss used to show how complete a driver he was. In fairness to Clark, I must add that his style of driving a saloon sideways, and fast, was even more impressive than Marshall's, especially when Clark has always maintained that he finds any kind of motor racing repetitively boring. How he could say that of the fantastically close racing he and Marshall indulged in on that 1974 Tour (all without a bent panel between them) is harder for me to understand.

As a racing driver Gerry has three outstanding strengths: his fantastic, but legal, starts (a legacy from his athletic sprinting prowess?); his ability to really make a race of a seemingly lost cause and his wonderful car control, especially in the wet, when I have seen him make the other big saloon car names look very slow indeed. His weakness could well be that car control for he cannot resist the chance to slide the car sideways at every opportunity and this can lose him time. In turn it can also lead to more than fair wear and tear on the car, though a man with his record in longer races, or with often fragile machinery, could never be dubbed a car breaker.

Off the track Gerry Marshall's interests are still dominated by high performance, on two or four wheels (via an embryonic collection scattered around Southern England). He is not particularly technically-minded, but has a brilliant memory for important changes in production specifications, engine power rating, performance figures, race results and other facts and figures that he finds interesting. He really has to be personally involved to show his intelligence in anything, which is one of the reasons why he never excelled at school, save on a running track.

His personality is normally pretty provocative in company. He'll make a seemingly pointless remark, delivered in the fast clipped style that's bred of high speed bargaining in the often ruthless world of secondhand car-dealing. What he has said is irrelevant, but the china blue eyes, slightly protuberant but as sharp and far-seeing as one would expect after all those hours at the wheel, will pick up any change in expression in the surrounding group, a quick, restless mind spitting out the real character behind the banalities often uttered in casual conversation.

That instant character analysis that he performs results in hilarious nicknames for well-known people on the motor-trading or motoring scene, all of them with a grain of truth that often hurts. Thus the respectability of an establishment name like the RAC's Neil Eason Gibson, the son of a famous name in motor sport organisation, becomes Neil Easy Gibbon; Sidney Offord becomes Silly Offals and some of the delicious ladies on the scene become unprintable!

As I said earlier, Gerry Marshall has been a columnist for at least three magazines, and this kind of humour is peppered throughout many of his contributions. The vintage examples are from *Cars and Car Conversions* through 1972: these were the result of unholy collaboration between the now-editor of that magazine (Terry Grimwood) and Gerry, usually using a tape recorder, though I have a typewritten sample in front of me. Headed "From the Hot Seat", it contains a stream of names that Gerry misconstructed within his September 1972 column, including Gillian Allaskew Thomas (actually a very neatly attired and determined lady driver, Gillian Fortescue Thomas); Tony Moskvich (that well known Lanfranchi driver); Peter Handsome (actually Hanson); Tony Drone (Dron); Terry Clanger (often known as Banger, actually Sanger!) and many more including the mangling of Walton to Warthog! The whole column that month was a particularly fine one, including Irish jokes long before they were in vogue: "Met an Irishman on crutches the other day. Told me he'd just tested the air brakes on his lorry by driving off Beachy Head. Ho Ho". There was also the story of a 1750 Alfa Romeo changing hands in exchange for a very plush 12ft caravan and five secondhand petrol pumps!

In recent years Gerry has turned to supporting an increasing number of other drivers on the track, mainly through his own Marshall Wingfield or *Mayfair* magazine spon-

Autosport Championship finale in 1966 with my Tuscan V8 leading Willy Green (Ginetta), Bernard Unett (Sunbeam Tiger) and John Miles (Elan). *Courtesy Mike Kettlewell.*

sorships. That activity points out the side of Marshall that is usually ignored, the sheer amount he puts back into the sport he supports. Not only do a number of drivers literally owe their place on a motor racing grid to his energy and enterprise, but he also appears at more club nights or forums in a week than most stars do in a year. He enjoys it, but when it involves travelling from Brussels to London to Scotland in a few days, even he admits it is hard work. But he will still turn up.

The saying: "Love him or loathe him, but you cannot ignore him", was made to cover the Marshall character. As ever with human nature things are a little more complicated than that. Having established that Gerry is a man of enormous contrasts and swiftly changing personality, let us look at some of the people and machinery that went to make up Britain's Mr. Club Racing.

Country boy

November 16, 1941 was the date of Marshall's debut which, for those who are interested in character analysis by astrology, puts him under the sign of Scorpio. As Gerry puts it: "My father was away fighting the German horde in the air force. The family home was in Brondesbury Park, which is sort of 'Kilburnish', but I didn't live there until after the War [his Dad was demobbed from the RAF in 1945] as my mother went to live with her parents and her brother, who was constructing airfields for Wimpey out in the country. So they had a house in Southoe, which is near St. Neots and Huntingdon.

"My father was at Cranwell but - so my mother always tells me - I was conceived at Sleaford, when my father was home on leave. They went away for a dirty, or clean as they were married, weekend!" Ask what Gerry's Dad did in the RAF and his eldest son gives the reply: "He shouted at people. Bullied poor unsuspecting airmen. In fact he was a Flight Sergeant and I remember my mother, long after the war, saying to him: 'You're not on the parade ground now, it's no use shouting at people!'"

The young Marshall, who was destined to be the senior of three boys, all spaced at seven year intervals, was born into a really rural atmosphere, but that sleepiness didn't prevent him from getting into some pretty lively scrapes. "I was always told by my parents that I was totally spoilt as a child, because I was living in my grandparents' house with a lot of doting relatives. There were a lot of females in the house; there was my mother, and the woman next door, Mrs. Ashford, she had two daughters. So I was thoroughly spoiled, it would appear!

"We didn't exactly suffer too much living in the country with the farm land and everything. One thing I can remember from many years ago - bearing in mind I was a total country boy - is from my Uncle Fred's farm, just up the road from us. One day I was wandering about when I came across the farm dump, where they collected all the old rubbish and so on, in a corner of the farmyard. I saw all these empty old cans of powdered milk. I came rushing back to the farmhouse shouting, 'Mummy, Mummy, I've found a cow's nest!' Even though I lived in the country I still believed it ...

"There was another occasion on the same farm when I managed to start-up this Caterpillar tractor. Now I had got into the habit of playing with the two tractors on the farm - both were non-self-starters: I used to pull all the knobs and press all the buttons and so on. They were both Fordsons, one was a Model A, I think, and I later learned to drive that around. That was great fun, because it had one of those clutch pedals that depresses to put on the brakes. Anyway, back at the Caterpillar, I found a knob on the floor that made a lovely whirring sound when I pushed it. Of course the bloody thing started ... and it was a diesel of course. I wasn't totally stupid, I was completely stupid! Diesels don't have an ignition to switch off, so I had this thing ticking over and couldn't switch it off. I was only five or six, so I had to rush back to the house and get hold of my father to turn this bloody thing off without giving me too big a walloping. It took about an hour to get up the courage, but I had to in the end. I've forgotten what happened now, I think he just stalled it".

Surrounded by all these mechanical toys - it was the levers and a lack of steering wheel that lured him into the Caterpillar incident, for they were even better to play with than those of the Fordson tractors - the toddler had little time for animals. Even today he says: "I like other people's dogs and things, but I'm not really bothered. I've always been crazy about things mechanical".

Gerry lived at Southoe and occasionally visited the Clifton's farm until he was six, but even after his return to the family house in North London, Gerry remembers returning to his grandparents' country setting for holidays. "I even had measles there. I used to love it; you know I used to cycle up to the farm every day and do a day's work up there. This lasted through when I was seven, eight, nine, ten ... up until they moved away, and that was when I was about twelve years old.

"I still like to work on the farm: I go up to old John Pope's place, when I have the time, even now. Then I used to love driving the tractor, for instance, and following the combine harvester going back-and-forth. I think, even in those days, I was always being told off for going too fast ... I was always a little bit too spectacular!

"The big thing in my life was, I remember, always being totally immersed in motor cars and motor transport. The highlight of the week was getting the local taxi into St. Neots on a wet day, because the buses ran so infrequently. There weren't many cars about anyway, so the occasion of the day was the arrival of the bus. It wasn't surprising that my first catch phrases were things like 'Here's bus, bus' and 'Tractor green, tractor blue', this covering the two Fordsons".

So far as cars were concerned Gerry's first memories are actually of, "... my father having a Jeep and coming home with his mate, who used to drop him off with us, then call and collect him after my father had spent some time with us".

The first contact with a motor car is vividly etched on Marshall's mind today, and his father also remembers the incident all too painfully. In Gerry's words here is the story: "My father was always talking about his car, which he had run for some time during the War, but when petrol became totally impossible he had to lay it up. He put it in the garage with his brother's car in Kilburn, near the shop, and unfortunately it was bombed, which didn't improve its appearance very much!

"It was an Austin Seven which in those days (it was a 1936 Ruby model) was quite a fair car. When I was about four or five, the great day came when I was taken to London town to see *the* car, I always remember this, and we walked up the long yard where this shed was and to where the car was kept. When he opened the door to the garage I burst into tears. I was quite expecting to see a Rolls-Royce, or something really smart, having heard all the stories of how they used to go on holiday in it, and so on.

"This thing, of course, had been bombed. It had been standing all over the War years as well, so it was covered in muck and all sorts: I was so disappointed! Even my father was a bit put out so he decided, going on pre-War values, that the car wasn't worth the trouble of repairing. He only paid £125 for it, brand new in 1936, and he went to Godfrey Davis to buy another car. There was an old Ford there, which was in as bad a condition as his Austin Seven, but they wanted £450 for it! So he suddenly realised that his Austin Seven was repairable, and he ran that for quite a few years actually. Never let us down, it was a marvellous car ...

"He repainted it - before the war, the car was beige and the family had always called the car the *Yellow Peril*. Another reason for the nickname was my father's driving, which was as erratic as it still is today! After the war he painted it green; in fact when he sold it, years later, he got his £125 back! He sold it during the fifties, after we had enjoyed many trips (including going down to Cornwall on family holidays and so on) and my grandmother was quite disgusted with him for getting so much money for it".

By this stage, the family were well established back in their ground floor home at

Brondesbury Park. This was despite a problem over a bombed-out family being moved in during the Marshall family's absence. Gerry recalls: "It was quite a nice little house, but my parents wanted to extend the family, so in 1947, when they had the bad winter, we moved to Kenton, Kingsbury, where we stayed until we moved on to Wembley, where my parents still are.

"It's quite funny actually: we are a sort of semi-Jewish family I suppose, and my father moved into the old St. Cuthbert's Vicarage, which he bought off the Vicar. Of course, Dad's main warehouse was a church! He actually bought a church, not bad for a good Jewish lad! In fact, one of the pews acts as a garden bench in my parents' garden nowadays", he added with mirth.

Gerry attended the local Kenton College, showing complete scholastic apathy, repeated at Harrow High School. At least his schooldays provided some firm friends who were to share his mechanical interests, and his friendship, into motor racing and to this day. He was interested in sport however, taking part in many sprint running events (a talent he still employs to this day, usually defeating any unsuspecting challengers, for the profit of himself and charity) and later becoming involved in rowing.

One of his firmest friends was Mick Leary, but it was Leary's father, Jack, who caught Gerry's attention. "Jack's a great character, drives you bloody mad, he does. He's Irish and he's an engineer, *and* he had the first ever Ferrari I ever saw. It was the ex-Tom Cole Ferrari, registered RGN 192. Jack and Mike would start it up outside his house and run it for about 10 - 20 minutes, getting the oil warm and making the thing fire on twelve cylinders before setting off up the road.

"The neighbours used to hate his guts, because a) he was fairly affluent and b) he was a mad bastard! I loved him, he was a great guy and, by a strange coincidence, he was one of the first to ever really develop a Vauxhall. He took the '52 Velox and bored out the 2.2 litre engine to 3.3litres, managing this by using the Bedford truck block, which was very similar anyway. It had overdrive on all gears, including reverse! He modified the suspension and everything; there was even an article on it in *Autocar*. It was very, very, quick for a Vauxhall, it really was. Jack was a bit of a good driver too.

"He always keeps threatening to show me this film he took showing these two little dots - of course I was a slightly fatter dot than his boy Mick - at the School sports. I was always able to run a bit, but I'm sure Jack wants to show the film for a more hostile audience than the Olympic selection panel".

In conclusion Gerry feels that his running was a bit like his sex life: "Short and sweet".

Another great schoolfriend was Roger Bunting and in talking about him Gerry Marshall is soon back with his real love, the internal combustion engine."Roger's dad had an MG Magnette, and before that lots of Jowett Javelins. In fact he was the Jowett distributor for the Home Counties at one stage: Bunting's Motor Exchange. All Roger and I wanted to do, and we both had this one ambition, was to own a Lancia Aprilia, which shows our taste can't have been too bad, for that's a classic car now.

"Roger had a Corgi scooter - remember we're talking about the early fifties now - and we used to muck about with that a lot in his garden. Anyway he did that up a bit and sold it: made a few bob on it in fact. Having made a profit, he then bought a Francis Barnett 197cc. I always remember that because the registration number was VNV 197. We used to come home from school, go round to Roger's house and drive like idiots all around. It was great, but we couldn't wait for him to be sixteen and able to go out on the road, and I would be able to do the same.

"And that's what we did, but my parents wouldn't let me have a bike, so I bought a moped. A fantastic machine, an NSU Quickly, the De Luxe version. It was just incredible, nothing broke on it, and we used to abuse it like anything, two up, anything at all and we'd be mad enough to try it at that age. That NSU was an incredible piece of German engineering". There's not a trace of a smile on Marshall's face when he recalls that moped

The 1256 Viva at a Cambridge University AC Sprint, Snetterton in 1967. You can see I had to huff and puff to make the car go at all!

Nick Faure in the ex-works Porsche 911 had to chase our Viva GT at one Brands: the Porsche spun eventually. *Courtesy Sunrise Universal Productions.*

Broken Minis and wet spectators are the background to this shot of me at the wheel of the original racing Viva GT at Brands. *Courtesy Colin Taylor.*

In 1969 we had our first TV win with the Viva GT. Note how big the crowd was in those days for the Gold Cup.

today. Obviously the chance to actually own his very own piece of mechanical engineering far outweighs memories of more exotic machinery that are his current daily repertoire.

However much he stood in awe of his first machine, there came a day when he felt he'd wrung every drop of performance supplied by the makers to a bareness that could only be relieved by more speed. The thought of Marshall and friend on an NSU, and a 200cc motorcycle, is quite frightening enough without the next step, which he recalls with his usual clarity for mechanical friends. "Then I got a BSA Bantam, a 150cc, which is the one up from the tiny one and down from the 175, the really quick one!

"Being me, I got one of our neighbours to machine the cylinder head and the barrel for me, which he did by being a good engineer and having a lathe. He raised the compression ratio and so on. Having done that it went a bit better. So having done it once, I decided to have it done a second time! And, of course, that totally ruined the whole thing. So, after a fortnight, that went back in on part-exchange.

I then got a new Panther with a Villiers 250cc two-stroke engine. That had Earles-type front forks, and was a very smart bike. After that I really gave up motorcycling, or rather motorcycling gave me up, for I had antagonised my parents so much they had to let me buy a car. I was seventeen when I had my first bike, a year older than Roger, and still in my teens when I gave it up". In fact motorcycles occupied only months of his' motoring life.

Gerry left Harrow High School at seventeen. His first job was at Maples, the furniture people who in Gerry's words were: "A much more staid, old family business than they probably are today. My father being a builder's merchant and ironmonger, I was apprenticed to the brass department, which is a polite way of saying 'ironmongery', I suppose. We dealt with all sorts of very posh people - Lord and Lady Sideways Duckshit, that sort of thing. I served my time there, but I just couldn't get any enthusiasm for the trade.

"The main problem was I just couldn't stand travelling on trains, I used to go to sleep. Having the motorbike was alright, but in all weathers it was a bit of a pain driving to Euston Road and so on".

Having mentioned his father so often, it is worth having Albert Marshall's recollections of this extraordinary War baby, and the background in which son Gerry was brought up.

Today Albert Marshall is an amazing contrast to his son. Where his son seems almost twice life size, Mr. Marshall senior is a smaller, dapper figure with a ruddy countryman's complexion and neat attire. His bright blue eyes look to be one of the few physical attributes he shares with his eldest son. The other sons are John, (born 1947) who has worked in the stores at Henlys, part of a chain of Leyland garages, in London, for many years, and Martyn (born 1954) whom Gerry describes as: "Sharing all my vices, plus one: he smokes!" Martyn does work for the family business, and has carried on the Marshall competition tradition.

Mr. Marshall senior represents the fourth generation of the family business, with an aura of respectability that is not accompanied by pomposity. As he succinctly puts it: "I spent five and half bloody years in the RAF, so I was pretty glad to get out in '45! Before the war I used to go and spectate at Brooklands and do the odd sprint, and I didn't really get involved in motor sports until I was 40 years old and a member of North London Enthusiasts Club. Before that I simply didn't have the money, or often the opportunity.

"So I did a few club sprints and driving tests and then I bought an MG and joined the MG Car Club. Going back to 1952, I used to take Gerald and John along to Brands Hatch when I raced the car, and Gerald would be allowed to drive the car up towards the start.

"As a ten or eleven year old Gerald would often be giving advice to people like Doc Shepherd and Don Moore at the track, and they used to listen politely to him. Imagine it, Don Moore listening to a kid. It was then I realised that he had to be a racing driver!"

Despite his father's fond remembrances it seems certain there was no question of Albert Marshall enthusiastically helping his son into competition. Indeed to this day he has never been to see Gerry compete. Although Marshall senior was quite well known in sporting circles he was not very keen on his young son getting involved in motor sport. Neither father nor son agree about details, but to an outsider it seems possible that Marshall senior's large accident in 1959, when he rolled driving a Magnette at Snetterton, may have altered the parental attitude to the sport. The fact that Gerry has introduced the youngest son to the sport as well, colours the memories of both parties with more recent disputes best left locked in the family cupboard!

We rejoin our hero at the age of 18, a momentous age for that is when he joined the Dealers Deliveries Ltd. concern and bought his first car. He started with the company in London: "... at the bottom. They then asked me if I would go as a kind of assistant to a new branch at Luton, at a place called Slip End, would you believe? Now it's the biggest car delivery depot in England, I think. I stayed there for the rest of my time with them, which was about two or three years. I really enjoyed working for them: my job wasn't driving vehicles but it was still very enjoyable. The winter we opened this depot featured mud and chaos: it was well-named Slip End, I'll tell you!"

That first car came almost simultaneously with the need to commute up the then new-fangled M1 Motorway to Luton every day. Naturally Gerry remembers it well, "... a Ford Popular, registered MTR 584, a 1954 model in upright perpendicular style. I bought it from Blue Star Garages in Belsize Park". This while working briefly at Dealer's Deliveries Abbotts Place, Kilburn, office.

"I remember it was the basic model to the Anglia. Dealers Deliveries did all the fleet moving for the Electricity Board and the Water Board, and they were replacing their fleet of Anglias, Prefects and Populars. We were taking them to the auctions. They'd often call into Abbotts Place and be left overnight for another driver to take them: that was how I got mine up to specification! All the latest goodies came my way - you know, chrome bumpers and vacuum tank for the wipers, it really was the poverty model. They used to give you those dreadful wipers, but no vacuum tank! That was a standard fitting on the Prefect. My car slowly came up to quite a good specification ...

"Over the years I did all sorts of mods to this car. It had Ballamy front suspension and, whilst I was in Luton, I came across Speedex at Windsor Street. They had Jem Marsh and Frank Costin (who was later to have quite an influence on my life) who had just started building the Marcos.

"I went to see Jem, and in characteristic style he managed to extract oodles of pound notes from me for my engine: the overall effect was that it didn't go any faster, but it was a lot more unreliable!

"The Popular used to have a great penchant for breaking its rear axle. This was because I always used to drive it on two wheels; when it came down, it used to virtually pull the diff out. I had about four diffs in a year! Other than that it was very good.

"At that time I used to knock about with Roger Bunting and John E. 'Edmond' Miles, the two of them apprenticed at Middlesex Motors. John had a Sprite, which we modified, and Roger had an A35 van with a really demon engine. I was as envious as hell. They had better cars, and there was just no way you could race the Popular - it was all I could do to keep it going on the road".

Not surprisingly Gerry was to end up with an A35 himself, but that was after an adult reunion with the sport. He went along to a Silverstone 8 Clubs meeting in the early sixties with his friends' cars, but with no prospects of driving as he was still comfortably under twenty-one and his father refused to give him permission.

"Roger had his A35 and went very well, I think he won a race with it. Graham Aylward was there in his TC MG - he went very well in that - another great friend of mine, Philip Morris, was there in his MG Y-type, into which he put a TF 1500 engine and called it a 'YF'. That was a great day, and we did the MG Car Club meeting a few weeks later, but

I always think a driver looks better with a face mask. I tried FF with a Lotus 61L ("L" for large!) in 1969.

Would you believe that's Emerson and Tim Schenken behind? You would believe anything then! I enjoyed the driving but found many of the drivers, umm, primitive.

Now, here's a picture of abject terror! Autocrossing in the Players No.6 Celebrity Moke, which had a quick 1300 motor *Courtesy Mauren Magee.*

I still wasn't driving. My father was very anti the sport, though he was still an RAC Steward and a member of the MG Car Club!''

Gerry's father was suffering from staff problems in the Ruislip Manor branch of his business. With great reluctance, and after a long and amicable chat with Dealers Deliveries' boss Jack Eastwood, Gerry left to join the Marshall business, where he worked for another three years. This was his last job before he became fully involved in the motor trade and competition.

Also in this early sixties period, Marshall finally exchanged the Popular for an A35, a car that led an action-packed life from the start. Gerry explains: ''I bought the car (10 CRO) from Barry Hall, a friend of Roger Bunting. I had it two hours and broke the crankshaft. The engine was rebuilt by Tim Conroy, who was then working at Speedwell: I never looked back from that moment on with the car - it was a never ending drain of money!

''I finished up with what must have been the fastest A35 on the road, at any time. I had things on that road car that even people who were racing didn't have. I had a ZF limited slip diff: nobody used them, they couldn't afford them, they used locked diffs. I bought all the remains of Doc Shepherd's A40 racer from Brian Claydon at Newtune, Cambridge. It also had the dubious distinction of being the first A35 with a 45DCO Weber on it, and I eventually also had one of the four high ratio steering boxes on as well.

''The car had quite a history. First of all it was Speedwell-tuned and it had been owned by Mike Butler, then a St. Albans local before he made his rallying and rallycross name: it was also owned by another local man who is now a member of the establishment and a JP. It's difficult to imagine him tearing around in that little Austin, but then he was a rep. for the same company that he is now controlling as managing director. Small world, particularly as he drinks in my local, the Six Bells.

''I was into everything at that stage and knew just who was doing what mods on the   *29* motoring scene. Most of the work was done by Brian Claydon at Newtune and I had the mechanicals on it from Shepherd's A40, UCE 13, plus a Weslake head and BMC 649 camshaft: all things that would be nice to get hold of today for Classic Saloon Car racing. It was about two years after A35s had been used in top level competition and there were lots of good bits around".

Turning to another favourite subject Gerry now feels he would have been motor racing earlier if it hadn't been for a woman. Which one of those was responsible, attracted by our youthful character's zest at the wheel - or when parked - seems a trifle confused!

What is certain is that the A35 was the first car of his that he used in competition, but that tale, and the amazing escapades in rental Minis and ever-ruder lady friends' machinery belongs in a subsequent chapter.

Before we leave our hero's early life, a cautionary story told in Gerry's inimitable style. "One Christmas we were all very raucous, doing silly things like drinking and driving and going everywhere like *hooligans*, yes it was very different then. It was actually Boxing Day and we had been to several good cocktail parties. Then, later in the evening, a very attractive blonde lady I was going out with and I ended up God knows where, and he knows why! Anyway I managed to fall over in the snow with the A35, right opposite my old school! I had to drag my father out to come and tow us in".

From the start it was obvious that Mr. Marshall's destiny lay in paths other than those of the dour introvert, springing from the hills to World Championship prominence.

Daring young man on the Mini scene

"John Miles and Roger Bunting were all still racing around me, but I'd discovered all about women ... or something about women anyway. So I hadn't got any spare cash, time, energy or even the enthusiasism to go racing! Funnily enough I was always frightened to race myself: I was always the team manager or procurer of parts, rather than the driver". Thus Gerry remembers how he did not go motor racing for what seemed such a long time to the impatient curly-haired teenager.

However that did not mean Marshall had stayed away from competition. As he tells it he was introduced to competition, first-hand, by a typically original method. "Lacking my parents' permission I didn't initially start competing with that A35, though I did eventually get around to it, as you shall hear in a separate sordid little story. What we did was find a firm in Wembley with a hire car business. It was called Hire-a-Car and we used to go down to them and hire Minis. These poor bloody Minis, we used to give them some 'stick'. We used to take them to Eelmore Plain, near Aldershot, and sprint them! I used to get seconds and thirds in the up to 1000cc class in rented Minis. That's actually how I started driving. We had some fun - Phillip Morris and myself and Martin Mulchrone [his best man later in life] ... Martin had his Zephyr Zodiac Mk II and he used to pound round too. Oh, he was Jack the Lad in that, I can tell you". Marshall and friends did several sprints in this way, even taking along such respectable devices as Wolseley 1500s to face the rigours of Eelmore Plain.

His second sprint was in an MGA fixed-head coupe. Now twenty years old Gerry was enmeshed in one of love's eternal triangle situations, but with a typically original twist: "I shared the MG drive with her husband! They'd had a row at this time and she'd gone off somewhere and I always maintained a good friendship with him as well ... very *strange* situation, I can tell you".

Some of Gerry's friends could see there was no future in such a domestic situation and they found him another, unattached, girlfriend whom Marshall recalls with equal relish. Her name is omitted too, but her physical charms and an age "over 25", were clearly great plus points in the Marshall of the time's mind. Everything went very well indeed and Marshall almost forgot about motor sport until: "... my parents went to Spain on holiday. I thought this was a good move on their behalf and decided to enter a sprint in my A35. It was September or October 1961 and the event was at Brands Hatch. I was up all the previous night, and I also polished the car nicely. I also borrowed the safety-belts out of my father's MG Magnette; bearing in mind belts were something of a novelty in those days, I find it a bit surprising how convinced I was that they were a Good Thing. It wasn't easy screwing out the full harness belts from the MG, I can tell you. Anyway, I managed to get them in and set off down to Brands Hatch and practised it. I think it was equal first in class on practice times, but I didn't get a run because I was a reserve entry.

"So I was very unhappy about all this, having been there all day, and I drove off for home. I was unbelievably tired, having been up all night polishing the car and all the tension and worry of what my father was going to say when he got back, if he found out. I got past Hyde Park Corner and was driving down the Bayswater Road and I literally dropped off to sleep ... smack ... into the back of a parked car!

"My girlfriend was also very tired and asleep, but she went forward and banged her head on a navigation light I had on the dashboard. The only funny thing about all that was that, at five or six o'clock at night, in full daylight at least two people came and said they saw the pedestrian run out in front of me. I thought that was quite good ... perhaps there was a pedestrian, but I did not see him, I'd just dozed off? That was the end of a beautiful relationship for a relative of the girl instituted proceedings against Marshall and love could not overcome the inevitable rancour stirred up by that move.

The A35's days were then numbered (though it had time for that snowy incident related in the previous chapter!) and Marshall's next mount was: "A Riley 1.5 in which two people had died". The Riley was bought from a friend of Gerry's father and rebuilt to a pristine finish.

Despite the Riley's morbid associations - and Marshall actually discredits himself by saying he is a 'ghoul' - few have done more to help set higher standards of safety. Of course, buying cars with such ghastly histories is unfortunately part of the motor traders life. Although never to compete in Marshall's hands, the Riley led him into motor racing ... but only as a car owner. The tale is circuitous but does eventually deliver a trembling twenty-three year-old Marshall to the starting grid. Here is how it happened. "At that time I was very heavily involved with Martin Davidson, who was later to race under the name Harry Martin. He had parental trouble like mine, but worse. In fact his parents belonged to a religious sect of lunatics who don't believe in anything you can enjoy. Martin, or 'Hairy Harry', as we used to call him, was training to be a solicitor. He had been generously indulged by his father in respect of cars over the years. Then when the Mini came out he decided he wanted a racing Mini and bought WER 113 an ex-Doc Shepherd car. His father thought he was buying an ordinary road Mini! When he got home of course, all hell was let loose. His father soon put the car up for sale in *Autocar*, but we bought it on HP before a buyer could step in.

"Martin wasn't allowed to race it, so we changed his name to Harry Martin and I was a partner in crime. He went to Brands Hatch and won his first race ... even got a lap record: very good indeed. However things didn't stay that bright for long. On another visit to Brands Martin was racing hard against the chap I bought the A35 from (Barry Hall) and, somehow or other, Martin went off at Paddock Hill Bend, wrote off the car and put himself in hospital. It was a terrible business and shook us all. After that it was bound to come out that he had been racing, and he stopped living with his parents and set out to make his own life. Somehow we repaired the car and converted it into a Cooper and Martin had a couple of good seasons, which were great fun".

Still Marshall was not racing himself, but all that changed at a Snetterton race meeting in 1963. "Martin had been racing the Mini in the wet, and he'd been beaten by somebody I reckoned should never have beaten him. That was only in my opinion, remember. I started drinking and laying down the law to him in the bar afterwards, generally being rude to him and telling him that I would have done better than that, if I'd been out there ... I wouldn't have been beaten and so on. There was a chap listening called Tim Farr, - a nice chap. He had been racing Minis in his first season. His car was an old one with two halves stuck together, a new 997cc Cooper engine and subframes fitted by Frank Hamlin, who worked at Newtune of Cambridge (a good New Zealand guy who went on to be Graham Macrae's partner in F5000). Farr's father had offered him a new Marcos if he passed his law examination and gave up motor racing. I presume Tim Farr's a millionaire by now, for he proved a very good dealer in that bar room session.

"The upshot was that I went home in a battered old Mini racing car and he went

Wrestling with Malcom Beake's Ford-engined Sprite in a local autocross. The owner knocked off the bonnet on some of the opposition!

home in my beautiful Riley! No money changed hands, but I couldn't believe it when I woke up and saw what I'd bought ... nor could my father. Having got this car I then had to do something with it, so I took it down to my father's shop and painted it. I did a couple of sprints in it and did quite well".

In fact an *Autosport* report of October 11, 1963 suggests that was absolutely correct. There's a picture of YCD 436, the Mini he bought in that Snetterton deal painted white and accompanied by the words: "Gerry Marshall attacks Paddock Bend with vigour on his class-winning run in his Group 2 Austin Mini-Cooper". The report itself described the battle for the class as: "... a walk-away win for Gerry Marshall" ... and is accompanied by said Mr. Marshall's initials at the end of the account! The meeting was a co-promoted Circle CC and BARC (SE) Brands Hatch Sprint.

Mike Kettlewell a journalist of the time, now a distinguished motor racing book editor, remembered Marshall as vividly in 1978 as he probably will in 2028. Then nineteen years old and working as a junior on *Autosport's* editorial side, Mike started meeting Marshall regularly in the Spring of 1963. Kettlewell says: "Gerry was still scarred from a bad road accident as a passenger in a friends A35 [In fact he still carries the legacy of a silver plate in his skull] and looked older than his twenty-two years. He was a mad keen enthusiast and the same could be said of his road driving. Frankly, it's hard to remember some of our meetings as they always seemed to end in my getting terribly drunk, usually somewhere in Kilburn.

"Quite regularly we would visit the Steering Wheel Club off Curzon Street and I *do* remember those evenings. The regulars included people like Bill McGovern, Mac Ross, and even Tony Lanfranchi must have appeared in this period, because it wasn't long afterwards that he reckoned publicly that he was the best club driver in Britain. Journalists like Eoin Young and Richard Feast used to gather there as well, and the whole thing generated a very enjoyable 'clubby' atmosphere.

"Gerry would turn up at the Wheel with advance copies of *Autosport* and would read the magazine from cover to cover, quite literally. He used to claim that he knew the names of everyone in club racing, and that's quite possible. Remember, there were only a few hundred then, and he was desperately keen. However, that doesn't mean he was ever boring: Gerry was always great fun to be with, especially in the club house after a race meeting".

Pulls like a train, handles as if on rails. The Viva in S&K days at Shepreth station with (left to right) Gerry Johnstone, myself, Bill Blydenstein and Don Hagger seated behind. *Courtesy LAT.*

Prior to his first race appearance, which was not until April 1964, Gerry carried on sprinting, but not always in his own car. He borrowed an ex-works Sunbeam Rapier for a hillclimb at Firle, beating the owner, but he didn't have quite the same fortune when he drove Bill McGovern's 1071 'S' at a Brands Hatch sprint in February 1964. As a contemporary *Autosport* account said: "Only the watches accused him (Marshall) of being slower ... It looked quicker! But then it always does if you go through Paddock in an any-moment-now attitude. Gerry got away with it ... ". The account went on to say how another did not, all before a TV audience as well. Things were a little different in 1964, were they not? There was a picture of Gerry in McGovern's Mini (CMK 855A) and reporter Ron Ambrose's description was shown to be wholly accurate as the Mini "... motored sideways all the way down the hill at Paddock, frightening everyone but himself", in the words of the caption.

Few drivers can have had their early careers as well documented as Mr. Marshall. Kettlewell, tongue almost lodged in his cheek, ascribes the wealth of material to: "The enormous number of whiskies Gerry bought me, and some other staff members of *Autosport* too!" Although Gerry ascribes the blame for his almost late (by his standards) entry into racing to women and his parents, it seems the weather was also to blame. His 1-litre Mini was entered at a March 1964 race meeting at Brands Hatch. He was quickest in his class again, but it started to snow and the 1 litre race, scheduled toward the end of the day's proceedings, was cancelled.

Later that same month Marshall had adopted the role of scribe/driver again when reporting the London Motor Club's Blackbushe Slalom. The account appeared in *Autosport* for March 27, 1964 and brings a couple of important technical features to light, so here is what Gerry said in his account of the Marshall Mini's performance that wet Sunday: "Fastest saloon car time came from Gerry Marshall's extremely rapid Newtune Mini-Cooper, now sporting a new 998cc engine and close-ratio gears. No less than twenty seconds behind in this class came George Maxwell's Baldyne-prepared car which, despite arriving on a trailer and making a fantastic noise, could not approach the Newtune car".

That account is even more interesting for the mention of that 998cc unit in the Mini (still YCD 436, but painted blue now). The acquisition of that unit was a major triumph in itself. Gerry was still entering Martin Davidson in the Marshall Mini, but the pair were no longer talking to each other as the result of yet another tangled love affair. How passionately they must have felt about that particular web can be judged from the fact that neither Marshall nor Davidson were direct participants in said affair, but since it involves people who are now happily married with offspring we will simply leave it that tempers ran hot. Meanwhile Marshall had seen, " ... the man in those days to beat was a chap by the name of Fitzpatrick ... John Fitzpatrick of course. He was winning everything in the 850, even in the 1000cc class. Then he converted his Mini to a 998. This 998 Mini-Cooper engine was in fact the prototype for the later Riley Elf 998 short-stroke engine. John had it a year before anybody else, and Ralph Broad was doing the preparation for him. It really was fabulous and he drove it very well too. So everyone wanted a 998.

"Now I was able to pull a few strings and get the Elf engine short block assembly via a friend at Abingdon. Brian Claydon built it into the car and it was finished about two hours before the Mallory Park Boxing Day meeting in December 1963. In the meantime; "Martin and I literally weren't talking, but I'd entered him for this race at Mallory Park in *my* car. I still wasn't driving mainly because I didn't think I was good enough at this stage. Anyway he had a fantastic dice with John Fitzpatrick in his Mini 998: In fact Martin led most of the race and Fitz beat him by about half an inch over the finishing line! That was the first time my car was raced while I owned it. So far as I was concerned it was the best race Martin ever drove, but we still weren't speaking.

"After that meeting I went up to Brian Claydon at Newtune. Brian had been doing all the labour on the car for nothing, and I told him that I was —— if I was going to sell the car after all this work had gone into it. I would drive it myself, but would he maintain 35

Martin Raymond and Terry Harmer (Mini-Cooper 'S' types) chase me in the one-off Imp drive I had for Alan Fraser - unfortunately the little flyer broke just before the flag. *Courtesy Sunrise Universal Productions.*

I drove Frank Costin's Amigo to a class win at Thruxton in 1971, our only appearance together. *Courtesy John. L. E. Gaisford.*

Rare picture of DTV-liveried Viva GT at Brands: they were both written-off at Lydden Hill within a month! I was driving my Firenza quite peaceably at the time. *Courtesy David Turney.*

it for me and I would pay for the parts? He said 'let's see how you go'. In fact Mrs Daphne Claydon was the one who made the decisions, a formidable woman but she had a heart of gold ... so long as you could find it! Anyway that was enough for me and I took the plunge: As I said, I'm not stupid, just totally stupid!"

The result was Marshall's first racing appearance in the 998 Mini at the Easter Monday Snetterton club meeting, a chilly start to the club racing season at that circuit. In terms of handling a Mini at speed Gerry had little to learn of course, having run in sprints and hillclimbs of varying types since those early rental Mini forays. That racing in company of other traffic, and respected opponents like Mac Ross in a similar Mini (BMR 10), did not bother him either was evident from the fairy tale result. He won the 1000cc class and beat Ross on a track that was drying out after a damp start to the day's proceedings. Snetterton became almost home for Gerry over the weeks following his debut. The following weekend he scored another class win in the 1 litre Mini. In a second race, on the same day, outright victory went to Norman Abbott (a name to remember) in a Twin Cam-engined 1600 Anglia which defines the era more readily than Gerry's race-long Jaguar playmate. Once again the Marshall Mini was to be seen in *Autosport's* pages, this time harrying the life out of Albert Betts in a 3.4 Jaguar saloon! Gerry remembers this well today: "... overtaking the Jaguar into the corners and then being repassed along the straights!" That event had actually been for saloon cars of unlimited capacity and Gerry took third overall, one better than in his earlier class-winning performance.

Although it was obvious that the young Marshall was something useful in the way of Mini pilots, even though there were an awful lot of young, and not so youthful, competitors around at the time. In fact, until financial problems sharply curtailed his first racing season, he won every time out, save for two unfortunate events. In the first of these a sticking carburettor needle left him fifth overall in an 8-lapper for 1 litre saloons. Just how close the racing was at the time can be seen from a contemporary picture showing winner Paul Layzell heading *four other Minis* in a bunch aptly described as a "Minimada" around the Riches curves, Gerry's car well-placed on the inside while three of the others are struggling along in rough formation outside!

Characteristically, having started racing Marshall wanted to keep at it every weekend. However, his poor luck persisted even when he ventured away from Snetterton. What would have been his fourth race was turned into just a painful memory. As Gerry says: "It was appalling weather for a BRSCC meeting at Mallory Park. It was miserable, with constant drizzle in the morning and bad visibility. Unfortunately I was a practice casualty, the Mini falling over at the hairpin, so there was no chance of a race".

Gerry Marshall and Brian Claydon staged a dramatic return, though. The following Sunday saw a series of 10-lap races held by the BRSCC in perfect weather conditions at Brands Hatch. Claydon's dedicated efforts completed the Marshall Mini by 10am on race morning. Gerry rewarded such whole-hearted support in the best possible way, winning the 1 litre saloon car event by twenty-two seconds (his first outright win) and breaking the lap record by 1.6 seconds, a very handsome margin indeed. Commentator Anthony Marsh, was moved to describe our hero as: "... a pacemaker amongst the Mini-men" - and that was no mean feat on his fifth outing.

Gerry continued his winning ways with the Mini-Cooper as long as his finances would allow. Today he remembers: "Halfway through the season I literally ran out of money, owing Brian for the parts and they'd done a couple of all-weekers repairing the car after I inverted it, so I owed them quite a lot of money. Also I had got engaged so I sold the car, bought an engagement ring [thus the quip about Carol wearing a Mini-Cooper on her finger] and gave up any ideas of motor racing".

Marriage
and mischief

"Having sold the Mini and bought an engagement ring, I wasn't what you could call terribly happy - but there wasn't much I could do about it. I then met this guy, Mike Walton (now heading the Weber carburettor operation in Great Britain) who was also having his car done by Brian Claydon of Newtune. He wanted to go Group 2 in 1965, but he hadn't got a car. So I bought a secondhand Cooper, less engine and gearbox, from a very dubious source! Then Newtune put in Walton's engine and gearbox, magnesium wheels, Weber carburettor and so on". Thus Gerry describes the deal that put him back into racing in 1965.

In 1964 Gerry was still working for his father, but 1965 brought him changes in just about every aspect of his life. The good news - and there are plenty of shocking revelations to come later - the good news of 1965 came on October 2, when he married Carol after an engagement lasting over a year.

The rest of 1965 was a stark mixture between some excellent sporting achievements, a new job within the trade and the loss of his driving licence for two years.

"In February 1965 I joined Brew Brothers in Kensington on the commercial-vehicle sales side. About three weeks after I joined the manager of the department left for Australia, bequeathing me his Hillman Imp and his job: I think it was the car - which we called the 'Hillman Limp' - that drove him to this.

"In April I went up to do one of the first Internationals of the year in the Mini ... *The Daily Express* event at Silverstone. The race itself was rained off after, in James Boothby's immortal words: 'we had all been strapped to our accidents'. For some reason Robbie Gordon and I had plenty of time to kill in the evening. So we had eighty-seven pints of beer in the Clubhouse; another thirty-thousand pints in the Green Man at Brackley and I was extolling the virtues of my company Imp, registered CYP 986C. For some reason I can't recall now we went back to the circuit and I took him out in the wet ... the wrong way round the circuit ... and then he did the same to me. The whole time I was holding in third gear on this desperately unreliable heap. Having done that we went back to the Green Man at Brackley, had a few more glasses of orange juice, and then I set off for home. I was going very quickly, as was my wont: after all I was a racing driver, and that's what racing drivers do, isn't it? That was my naive theory in those days. I'm charging along, and come upon a lefthander on the main road into Towcester, before the Roade junction. I go flying into it doing all the clever things one does. You know, waggling the wheel and pushing up and down on the pedals, and generally acting the goat, when it just jumps out of third gear and falls over!

"The car is now upside down and looking very unpretty. I'm not at all amused by all this, obviously. It's all a bit unfortunate, but then a couple of chaps in a Cortina stop and push it onto its wheels. Wonder of wonders, the thing still went. In fact it was such a horrible car, I don't think it made much difference to it!

I drove it home without a windscreen but there was a snag. The people who had picked it up so kindly for me were members of the local constabulary, off-duty. On their way on-duty they had to report what they had seen". That would not have been so terrible in itself, but in Gerry's efforts to extricate himself from the mess with his employers he made things a lot worse, the written-off Imp bobbing back into view after it was meant to be dead, buried, or stolen. That led to a considerable court appearance, the loss of his licence (though not his competition licence) and the job. All enough to cheer anyone up who was about to get married six-months or so later.

Employment was swiftly solved however. One of his constant drinking companions at the Hereford pub in Kensington had been Squadron Leader James Boothby (Ret), every inch as much a character as Gerry himself. Boothby was: "... the Boothby-Gordon Partnership enthusiastic purveyors of new and used TVRs, in those days, though Robbie Gordon had left and John Wingfield was semi-involved. John had lots of business interests and 11 Reece Mews, a home of ill-repute to unemployable racing drivers and motoring characters, was one of them. Also around at that stage was Martin Lilley who used to waste everybody's time permanently, but he did form Barnet Motor Company, which had some business dealings with Lotus".

Before we get too involved with Barnet Motor Co. and the important part that organisation was to play in Gerry's business and sporting career, we will return to the Mini Cooper 'S' that Gerry was to share with Mike Walton. "Unfortunately his engine went bang quite early", Gerry now recalls, completing that car's history, "before I even drove it, in fact. So we had to get an 'S' engine and I bought one that had belonged to the dreaded Terry Hunter. It had been standing in Don 'Quack' Abrahams' front drive in Northwood, encased in a big Austin 1100, for two years.

"We built that into a 970 'S' a change of crank and rods, plus an increase in bore of 40-thou gave us 990 cc. This we used for Group 2 and club racing because we had some glassfibre panels from the previous year and a bonnet that would take a downdraught Weber instead of the twin SUs for Group 2.

"The only snag was, Mike and I weren't exactly hitting it off: he was quite a bit slower than me and there were the inevitable hassles over splitting up the wear and tear bills. So Robbie Gordon lent me the money needed to buy out my half of the car. I had a super season in both categories, culminating in beating Fitzpatrick in the works 970 'S' at Snetterton in an early round of the British Touring Car Championship. It really was good".

Of all the good placings scored in that car, April's Snetterton international must have compensated a lot for the bother that was to ensue from that ill-starred Silverstone meeting. It seems amazing to recall days when Snetterton reverberated to battles between names like Graham Hill, Jim Clark, Jackie Stewart and Jack Brabham, but they were the headline news on April 12 1964, all battling for Formula 2 honours. The pace in the saloon event seemed as frenetic. Reporters of the period commented how the tyre war was developing throughout the grid ("The works Minis were fitted with green spot Dunlop R6s", wrote one such observant scribe!) and gave a long account of the event, which separated the two halves of the F2 race. While Mike Salmon took the Dawney Racing/F. English Ford Mustang to victory and Jim Clark struggled with an out-of-sorts Lotus Cortina, Machiavellian proceedings were taking place amongst the tiny tots. At that time John Rhodes and Paddy Hopkirk had the 'senior' 1.3 Mini-Cooper 'S' types, the Irish rally star charged with the duty of pulling Warwick Banks along in the works-backed 970 'S' Mini-Cooper in the 'junior' team car. That put Banks well out of reach of a furious battle between the other works Cooper 970 'S' of John Fitzpatrick and G. Marshall Esq. The *Autosport* reporter even commented that the towing tactics were reminiscent of the 1960 Monza GP, which shows how seriously they took saloon car racing at the time! After all the drama was over Gerry had scored one of his most cherished placings ever, beating Fitzpatrick in the works car and pushing himself into the limelight in which people took him a lot more seriously.

As usual in 1965 Gerry had quite a few outings at Snetterton, but one at the beginning of the year showed his devotion, and another in August a new partnership. In March 1965 he was at Snetterton driving a borrowed, but standard, Mini-Cooper 1071 'S' in the Cambridge University Automobile Club Sprint, this time writing his report under his wife's maiden name of Maynard! By August he had been forced to sell back the 990 'S' to Robbie Gordon, who subsequently sold it off to one Julian Hasler.

The new partnership at the August Snetterton 500 kilometre race (a round of the European Touring Car Championship that year) had come about thus: "Robbie (Gordon) had also bought the ex-Trevor Taylor/Anita Taylor Aurora Gears 1275 'S' Mini-Cooper built by Alexander Engineering. I drove that with a mutual friend of Robbie and myself, David Wansbrough, an interesting gent who used to drive Lister and D-type Jaguars, and who was also the son of George Wansbrough, founder of Gordon Keeble Cars and former chairman of Jowett. If you managed to follow that, you may also be interested to know that we drove that car, further modified by Newtune, in the 500 kms and wonder of wonders, we won the class", Gerry relates. For nearly four hours' racing the little Mini had averaged over 72mph and beat the Janspeed car of Geoff Mabbs/Andrew Hedges, plus Vic Elford and Laurie Goodwin. Both the last named crews and Tony Lanfranchi (who led the category for over half the race distance) suffered mechanical troubles, but it did show the unexpected aptitude of this sprint runner and driver toward longer distance events.

The year was not free from controversy on the track. A Group 2 outing with the 1-litre Mini-Cooper at Crystal Palace led to some criticism of his driving in June. However an unbiased spectator wrote in defending Marshall's run to a second in class placing behind Fitzpatrick's Broadspeed Mini, and the fuss faded into a correspondence column controversy.

Gerry's stay with James Boothby was only a matter of months before Martin Lilley invited him to manage Barnet Motor Co., this move leading him into numerous Elan and TVR racing and sprinting appearances. Even now Marshall has no doubts about how the company came to be formed: "People say Martin did it all as a business investment, but that's all bullshit. Boothby had convinced Lilley of the value of £2000-worth of TVR shares *and* sold him a TVR Griffith V8, which Martin soon damaged heavily. Two weeks later TVR cars went into liquidation, so Martin Lilley not only had a TVR that he'd written off and couldn't have repaired, but shares in a company that gone bankrupt!

"As a face-saver Martin bought TVR Cars and formed TVR Engineering. It was done, not as the gallant saviour of TVR, as many say now, but because Lilley wanted his racing car back: in fact it was the only way he could get it back ... and that's all he was interested in! Martin bought the shares, and acquired quite a lot of debts, but it's as well to remember that £2000 was worth rather more than it is today. In fact I'll always remember, even when we reformed the company a TVR Griffith V8 was only £1695". One car that did not reach the showrooms was the TVR Tina; these Imp-based prototypes named after Marshall's eldest daughter.

"Now Martin had also bought himself a competition Lotus 26R Elan that year, but that lightweight Elan wasn't ready until the end of '65. That was my original Elan - I nearly always drove it - unregistered, but we labelled it BAR 1. An 1865 cc version of the Ford Twin Cam engine had been ordered, but that was a total disaster and we didn't actually run it in the car. There was even a court case over that (which we won) but Jackie Oliver had been running an Elan very successfully, done by Expert Engineering at Ware. So we went along to them and they did us a 1650 cc version of that original engine, using the standard crank and rods. We called these the 'rubber crank and rods', and I would only use 6500rpm. That led to the nickname 'Six-Five Special'. That was a fabulous car

41

This was my first new road going Vauxhall. Here it is sprinted at Brands Hatch just before sale in 1971. *Courtesy Dave Knowles.*

I took my Firenza road car out for a thrash in the 6 Hour Relay Race in 1971. This car was well-modified and covered quite a few competition miles. I wonder if its ever been sold as: "Never raced or rallied etc ... "! *Courtesy Colin Taylor.*

Run Baby Run - but not fast enough here! The man in black (Dave Brodie and his Escort) and my white Viva engaged in many such scraps - here we are unusually far apart! *Courtesy Harold Barker.*

An upstart South African chases me at Crystal Palace. Jody Scheckter pursues my golden Mexico during my 1971 championship year in the category.

and won practically everything it ever did in its original form ... FTDs, race wins and God knows what. I had no intention of driving it originally, it was really for Martin, but it was so easy to drive. In fact the first race I did with it [the Lydden Hill event referred to later by DTV boss Bill Blydenstein] I got the lap record, which still stands because they changed the circuit at the end of the following year".

It was actually the first year that Lydden Hill had been open for motor racing and Gerry was involved in quite a fracas on the way to that record (39.2 seconds/64.74mph.) On the front row were Keith St John (driving an Elva for the people who had pulled in such a large audience for the meeting, wonderful Radio London), Gerry in the Elan and Chris Meek with a Ginetta. As ever Meek had been involved in a season-long controversy over his competition habits, but he had reckoned without the Mini-bred Marshall. Gerry recalls this October 24, 1965 meeting today: "Chris Meek and I had a coming-together. He was in the works Ginetta and we hit each other on the first corner; I just held my place and he went off, catapulted all over the place and wrote the car off. It got lots of beers bought me by John 'Diva' Miles, who had the same thing happen to him, but the other way round, at Cadwell Park!

"I think the best thing I ever did with the Elan was at a Boxing Day Brands, closing 1965. I started from the front row of the grid, but so did David Piper in Dan Margulies' Ferrari 250 GTO, the most beautiful Ferrari you've ever seen. The flag dropped and I schlepped off into the lead for a couple of laps! David Piper went by (after three laps to be exact) and then I got by him and eventually he got by me by actually nerfing me out of the way. He really had to work in the GTO around Bottom Bend. I really reckon I would have been by him again in another lap, and there were only 10. What was really nice was that he came up to me after the race and said I'd driven fabulously, which made my day more than anything; we went down to the pub together afterwards". In fact Marshall gained the fastest lap and was very much the heroic David of Goliath ilk in contemporary reports.

For the 1966 season the Elan story was not so bright, but Gerry had the compensation of having already made the acquaintance of the type of car that was to serve him so well, right up until he left Barnet Motor Co. in 1967, the 4.7 Ford V8-engined TVR Griffith. The Elan saga went sour with the arrival of a new car, though many thought it was the original as it was still 'registered' BAR 1.

Gerry tells the full story as follows. "We thought it deserved a good engine. That was the mistake of a lifetime, of course. Expert Engineering were paid a lot of money to produce us an engine based on some other prototype work they had been doing with Ford's five-bearing motor. These were short-stroke 1300 and 1500 engines, so they did me a 1500 short stroke Twin Cam, with dry sump lubrication: in fact, I think I had the first Elan with a dry sump set-up.

"We thought our previous car had been so successful that we could sell it, minus engine and gearbox, and buy a new one from Lotus and have the new engine. So the car was duly sold, and the new one painted the same colour as the one before. The engine was another disaster, and never worked. It also ruined Expert Engineering eventually and some of their chaps ended up working for us. That car didn't do a lot of good. You could do a bit, then the head gasket or something would blow. We entered the *Autosport* Championship in 1966, the year John Miles won in an Elan-Willment. Then I wrote off the car in a sprint at Brands Hatch, which is another story about Peter Deverell's wedding that will remain untold.

"It was rebuilt, but I didn't want to race it again after that, I'd really lost interest in the car". Barnet Motor Co. put John E. 'Turner' Miles into the car for a couple of events, but still it wasn't getting results. It was eventually sold around the time Gerry left the company, in 1967. The man who bought it was killed in his first race with the car ...

At first the TVR Griffith MMT 7C was kept employed mainly in sprints and like events, but in 1966 more serious preparation took things to the point where Gerry might

Champion! The Escort Mexico and I won the Ford series in 1971. *Courtesy David Turney.*

The late lamented Crystal Palace circuit. From left to right: Gerry Johnstone, myself, Blydenstein and (seated) Dick Waldock. We practised the Firenza for the first time at this 1971 meeting, but raced the Viva GT shown.

Happy dicing with Mike Chittenden's remarkable Anglia in late 1971. *Courtesy David Turney.*

confuse onlookers by turning up at a small sprint with a normal roadgoing TVR, or racing with a car that was gradually developed during the season, especially in respect of the braking and improved halfshafts to cope with Gerry's inevitable sideways antics. Naturally, Gerry recalls the car with his usual clarity and how it began life. "I remember driving Martin Lilley's Griffith back from its rebuild with an extra-heavy body! Such was the way of TVR Engineering in those days, it had originally been fitted with a sunroof, but they filled that in with glassfibre too.

"I started driving that, and it was really more my style, I did lots of races with that, we never touched it, the Griffith was just dead reliable. It was a lovely car, and I raced it through 1966 and 1967, up until I left Barnet Motor Co., in fact. They always did use a 4.7 engine, and we used to race it in the heavy duty, solid-lifters, form when it had a claimed 271bhp. I remember I did acquire the single-multiple choke Holley carburettor from Mike Salmon's successful F. English Mustang, but apart from that it remained surprisingly standard on the engine side.

Apart from scoring umpteen race wins and FTDs in the Griffith, I also did Tholt-y-Will Hillclimb, where we got in the top-ten with it: I think we got FTD at every sprint we ever did with the competition version. I even did a round of the Player's No.6 Autocross Championship, sharing with the TVR autocross ace, John Akers. The event was at Elstree, near the company, and we got first and second fastest overall on a very muddy day, when even Minis were failing to get round the circuit. Our fastest time was 17-seconds better than the rest, and that was a racing car!

"The first time I drove a Griffith was back up at Eelmore Plain, in a sprint, I did the report for that one too - and I also drove an Elan on the same day. I decided I preferred the TVR of the two road cars. The TVR was more controllable on the throttle: it was a very tight little circuit and, I suppose, having driven round there sideways and backwards, and God knows what, the logical progression was to take it onto a track, with racing tyres. The beauty of the TVR Griffith was it had an enormous *range* of power: it would go from 3500rpm to 7200rpm. Mind you, it had one of those electric Smiths rev-counters in, and everyone said it would have gone bang twenty-thousand miles before if we really had been using seven-two! That TVR would pull seven-two on the tachometer going down the old Norwich Straight at Snetterton: we used to reckon that was 150 plus mph. It was a fabulous thing, dead reliable too, but it wouldn't stop!"

Gerry's first race in a TVR was undertaken in John Wingfield's ex-Paddy Gaston Mk 3 1800 (carrying a 'number plate' XPG 1) in a round of the Redex Championship at Brands Hatch. All went well, very well in fact, and Gerry finished third overall in a race won by John 'Diva' Miles. Martin Lilley soon offered to let Marshall loose in his Griffith. Driving such a variety of cars during 1965 it was perhaps surprising that Marshall was able to score enough points to take second in class in that year's Redex Championship, his first notable appearance in any championship series points tally. In 1966, on Boxing day at Mallory Park, he added another TVR victory to his total in Tommy Entwistle's 155bhp Mk 3 with stretched 2-litre MGB engine.

His fondest memories are of the Tholt-y-Will hillclimb in the Isle of Man. Marshall's enthusiasm was also shared by the *Autosport* staff of the period who regularly requested the annual September event's inclusion in the European Hillclimb Championship. Lancashire AC's organisation attracted a lot of favourable comment, but it was the smooth surface of the 3.6-mile challenge (part of the TT course, between Selby and Bungalow) that many liked, as well as the variation in corners from ess-bends to hairpins throughout the hillclimb course, which had a minimum width of 16ft and a maximum gradient of one-in-five. Gerry's finest performance came in Septemember 1966 when he took the Griffith up in third fastest time on the initial runs, and retained fifth place overall amongst the hillclimb specials (which then included the four-wheel-drive BRM for Peter Westbury) at the end of the day.

Gerry also had, "... an 1800S TVR Mk3 demonstrator registered LHV 41D. Lovely

47

Lined up, ready for debut of Firenza in a race at Llandow, South Wales.

car, with seventeen coats of paint, it was the first *proper* car Martin ever had produced from TVR Engineering. We decided that I really ought to do some racing in that as well as the Griffith. In fact I think the Griffith was just about to become a Tuscan: they were going to change the badges! So Martin bought Tommy Entwistle's crossflow-headed 1.8-litre MGB engine for the car. David Hives, known as 'Ferrucio' at the TVR factory was responsible for the preparation. It was a really heavy car, complete with radio and everything.

"We ran that car in the BOAC 500 at Brands Hatch in 1966. For a co-driver I had that shy young driver, Lanfranchi: I think that was the first time we actually drove together. We were doing really well, there may have been Johns Hine and Miles in Elans, but of course they were non-finishers - I always said Elans never could finish a short race, never mind a long one! Anyway we had the class sewn up, and we would have been very well placed overall too, even though we had the clutch slave cylinder go - we just drove clutchless through the pissing rain. Super race [he yawns reflective at the memory] then, fourteen minutes from the end the bloody wheel fell off. Good old TVR halfshaft failure..." Gerry, Tony Lanfranchi and Innes Ireland (whose GT40 had failed him while leading) then, "... repaired to the bar and got extremely nasty".

When the car was returned from its delayed rebuild it made an extremely effective class-winner in marque sports car events, notching up many such victories. There's another story about this TVR and the racing Griffith that shows even the ebullient Marshall at a rather low ebb. "We only had the one trailer, which we used for the Griffith, preferring to drive the 1800S on the road. That reminds me of one disastrous six-hour Relay Race we did at Silverstone, also in 1966. Oh yes, we were very into motor sport in those days at Barnet Motor Co. ... that's probably the reason we never made any bloody money. I digress, I did the first stint in our Griffith and we were doing very well, right up front with this thing on the road (it's a handicap event) when the inevitable happened. The damn wheel fell off. I abandoned that at Becketts and ran back to the pits to hand over the sash to the team, which nearly killed me.

"The team carried on and I then went to the bar and had a couple of glasses to recover. They then put me out again in my 1800S, I did about 1 1/2-hours running on the big tank. Then, at Woodcote, a wheel fell off. I spun round, didn't do any damage to the

The Firenza in its first race on the way to a new Llandow record in September 1971. We also did the sports car race that day, and won that too! *Courtesy Vauxhall Motors.*

car. So I crossed the track and ran up the pit road again! This time was a bit different though because I knocked over John Gott [now deceased but a former Chief Constable of Northamptonshire and an excellent Austin Healey driver] which can't have been much fun for either of us, especially him!

"However, I got back to the team again, passed the sash over to team-mate Peter Simpson and that was that, I thought. Unfortunately I went to the bar again and celebrated rather more well than wisely! Now, we had a Humber Super Snipe tow-car and trailer for the Griffith. So I went out from the Clubhouse and put the now-repaired Griffith back on the trailer and drove the *équipe* back through the pits and knocked both blanking wheels off the trailer against the pit counter!"

The weeks following that BOAC 500 were pretty eventful ones for Gerry. He had actually only just got off the boat on the Isle of Man, to attend what was a very successful Tholt-y-Will Hillclimb for him, when he heard that Carol had borne their first child, Tina. Another pleasant surprise was when Bill Blydenstein let him have a couple of laps in his demon lightweight 850 Mini at Snetterton. "I was up there to test the Griffith and I didn't realise what an honour it was when he asked me to try the car. That was in the days when there was a hairpin at Russell, which meant going down to first gear in this Mini. It had no torque at all, it was a super screamer and I was really half frightened of it, because a FWD car with an LSD and no torque is a totally different kettle of goldfish to a TVR 4.7 with no brakes and no roadholding all driven on the throttle.

"I thought no more about it afterwards, but obviously Bill was sufficiently impressed with me to offer me the car for sale at a later date". In fact Gerry bought the car on a shared basis with Ken Ayres in 1967, the year he was to leave Barnet Motor Co. and start working on his own account. Ken Ayres didn't get on too well with the car, being stuck with wetted plugs more often than getting a good clean outing, but Gerry had four races in it, securing the lap record for the 850 class (which stood for 2 1/2-years) on his first outing at Snetterton, and taking class wins. When Marshall left Barnet Motor Co. he sold his share in the Mini not feeling that he could afford to race that year, as well as set up his own business too. The money was needed *chez* Blydenstein, for they were putting together a Viva that would later cross the Marshall's then-changeable life. In his words: "I formed a company with Bruce Duncan and Martin Maudling to make all sorts of glassfibre parts   *49* for MGBs, but that never really got off the ground so I started trading from home, though it was very difficult with such a lack of capital."

That lack of cash showed in another story from 1967, one that was also to yield happier news in the following year. Marshall went up on his annual September visit to the Snetterton 500kms again, having failed to secure a ride with Barrie Williams in 1966. He'd won his class in 1965, as we recounted. Making the rounds of the Mini teams, he encountered Rexford Finnegan, an American with a Mini 1275 'S' prepared by John Aley. "I bullshitted this American into thinking I was a guarantee of success, just sitting in the car. I practised it something like twelve seconds a lap faster than him, which doesn't tell you anything about my driving, but does say a lot about his! So I did the start of the race, but after half an hour it had a common problem of the time, the Diva bush went and oil seeped onto the clutch and that was our race run. The American had two great mechanics working for him and he was talking about an assault on the European Touring Car Championship for the following year, taking in all the European tracks. If it hadn't been for Rex, I would never have seen places like Monza and so on".

Who says you can't do it in a Firenza? Famous personality is quite safe on the Motor Show stand as I search for a brochure, or something, to reveal the racing Firenza's vital statistics. *Courtesy Lynton Money.*

This shows the standards of preparation Old Nail actually displayed - despite its affectionate nickname. All Bill's cars were beautifully presented. *Courtesy Vauxhall Motors.*

Blydenstein Power

Relief might well be the word to describe Marshall's feelings when Blydenstein rang him up in the Autumn of 1967 to ask Gerry in a roundabout fashion if he would demonstrate the Viva in front of the Shaw and Kilburn top brass, and give a second opinion on it. Since he had no job, a wife with one child and another expected, and above all nothing to compete in, it was a very welcome phone call.

Blydenstein describes his view of that session in the next chapter, but Gerry's impressions were as lucid as ever to end this section of his pre-Vauxhall career.

"I went to Snetterton and drove the car for the first time (then with barely 80 bhp and 1258cc engine) and it was a nice day", he records blandly before adding the meat. "It handled very, very well: nice and flat after a TVR Griffith. Also, of course, it was totally and utterly gutless! I mean it wouldn't even stay with a 1300 Mini in a straight line, but it *handled*. The other thing I remember was, when you changed down to third the rev-counter went berserk because we had a limited slip differential that was more suited to a lawn mower". As an afterthought it should be noted that Marshall was equally impressed by the offer of a princely £10 a race. Yes, there was no doubt about it, he was on his way ...!

DTV and the people behind it

"The first time I really noticed Gerry Marshall as a driver was during mid-summer 1966 at Lydden Hill. We were still using the short circuit and I remember winning the 850 race in my Mini, setting a new lap record at 42 seconds. Gerry was there in his Lotus Elan and I marvelled at his car control. As it happened I was standing next to Carol Marshall, then shortly expecting their first child. I remember saying how I thought it was worth coming a very long way to see him in action". These were the words of Dutch-Norwegian 'Billy' Blydenstein, who was to become the architect of a new wave of success for Vauxhall, though he was not to know that when he and Marshall first met. Or that the two of them were to provide nearly a decade of entertainment and success for the British public. However, Bill's first encounter with the Marshalls was at a Brands sprint in 1958: it was Blydenstein's first event, and he won the class, which also featured Gerry's dad.

As Gerry has recounted, all sorts of unlikely people have done all sorts of unlikely things to Vauxhalls in the years since the Luton marque passed from being one of the prestige Edwardian and Vintage era sporting names to the British producer of General Motors family saloons. Sporadic attempts had been made to get the company back into competition. Blydenstein had been involved, racing a VW 4/90 loaned to Chris Lawrence in Europe as well as supplying a special cylinder head for the VX 4/90 rally team of 1963. This works-backed team was withdrawn after one member was killed and Bill's attention switched to Minis, a subject where one could hardly miss Marshall in the mid-sixties.

In 1966 Gerry first drove one of Bill's cars, the de-stroked 850 Mini referred to in the last chapter, which was pulling a raucous 8600rpm in testing at Snetterton, the Norfolk track that has played such a large part in both their careers. According to Bill, Gerry came in after his allotted few laps "bubbling with enthusiasm, commenting that this was the best handling Mini he had ever driven. As it only weighed 9.5cwt, and Gerry always did have a low centre of gravity, it was perhaps not surprising!" Bill's spry figure shook with laughter behind his tiny attic office desk at Shepreth when he told me this. One of the reasons he and Gerry were able to stay together so long was simply that Bill is a gentleman, with a manner and humour that bears no malice. Any harsh Marshall critic would have seen our normally cheerful hero heading for the door, surrounded by a cloud of fearful obscenities.

Gerry ended up buying that Mini, of course and it was very successful. As Bill recalls: "It was a sight for sore eyes. He seemed to fill it complete, sides bulging ..." The normally sober Blydenstein is reduced to almost helpless mirth at the memory.

More seriously, Blydenstein was looking for something to do "instead of shoehorning engines in and out of Minis". That something was actually a formal letter to Vauxhall, investigating the chances of competitive co-operation in their products. He had been sprinting a bored and stroked 1258cc HA Viva, winning class awards at Woburn hillclimbs and so on. Bill read in *Autocar* what a great advance the curvy HB model represented over the HA, and how the roadholding might be compared to the progress that the Mini originally established over its opposition.

Because of the GM non-competition policy at the time, it is hard to pick up exactly who at Vauxhall went out on a limb and suggested that a little support might be un-officially applied in an effort to overcome the somewhat stodgy image of the period.

Remember, this was long before Dealer Team Vauxhall was formed, (that was in 1971) so the idea would need some persuasion to pursue. An exceptionally articulate marketing man who was involved at the start, and who continued to push the competition cause all the way to the top at Vauxhall was Jeremy Lawrence. He was then manager of product information and still recalls the '66/'67 Christmas meeting with Blydenstein that led to, " ... very limited support". Now working on the truck promotion side of the company, Lawrence could be described as the architect of DTV as an established team, rather than the nuts and bolts, which have always been Blydenstein's responsibility. Today there are 650 Vauxhall dealers contributing to the team's finances. That it should be so successful owes something to the efforts of many on the dealer, DTV and Vauxhall sides: but, I think special credit should go to founder chairman Alan Maidens, who was also a big, amiable man.

Another Vauxhall man who was in at the start, but who is still associated with liaison for Shepreth today is Colin Wood, a senior project engineer within Vauxhall's huge engineering and styling department. Wood was concerned in the 1963 Vauxhall rallying effort, so it was natural that he and Blydenstein should talk again. Nowadays Gerry Marshall dubs Colin as part of 'Bill and Ben the Engineering Men'. The second character, Ben, is actually Roy Cook, the DTV liaison engineer since 1973 and subject to many Marshall stories on the theme: "The most frightening drive of my life was following Roy ..." A somewhat indirect link, from the Vauxhall viewpoint at least, was also established direct between Graham Curry, now a senior Vauxhall project engineer on trucks and the projected new team. Curry shared the Viva in the early days and proved a fine driver. He was also a near neighbour of Gerry's so Marshall had more than one way of knowing exactly what was going on at Luton. Wood and Cook both feel that Curry's efforts have always gone uncredited because they were unofficial, but nevertheless he got the message across inside the building that a Vauxhall was back in competition. Later on, of course, there was fantastic work from talented individuals on the styling side of Vaux-hall.

Depending on whom you talk to, the Shaw and Kilburn special, the original push-rod engined Viva HB, was either a convenient label or the sole result of S&K's interest in the sport. Be that as it may, Blydenstein started work on the car from his double garage at Therfield, near Royston. He was joined by Han Akersloot, a Dutchman who was to race the car as well as help on the mechanical side.

A press release on March 31 1967 had a picture of the car and the bare details that Akersloot and Bill Blydenstein had completed the initial testing of the 80bhp car of 1159cc, but by then the car had already made its debut.

In *Autosport* dated March 3 1967 Simon Taylor reported the competition debut. "Sensation of the 1300cc class was Billy Blydenstein's new Viva ... despite a lot of sideways motoring round the bale at Sear its first run was nearly 2.5 seconds quicker than that of the next man up". The results had the following coincidence "BTD: G.D.R.Marshall (4.7 TVR Griffith V8) 55.75s ... Class winners: W.B.Blydenstein (1.2 Vauxhall Viva) 61.55s". The venue was at Snetterton and the event was Cambridge University Automobile Club Sprint.

It was a fine debut, but Bill's relationship with Akersloot suffered through the following season - despite a move to slightly more spacious premises at Bassingbourn - for it was hard going trying to develop the power train into a reliable and competitive unit. Bill was also puzzled that Akersloot wasn't lapping below two minutes at Snetterton.

Wonder if they've got a spare wheel? Second such incident in a Magnum at Brands, happily a mite less frightening than the first. *Courtesy V. R. Langrish.*

Blydenstein decided to take a personal look at the problems and, accompanied by his first employee (Don Hagger), he tested the car at that track, lapping in a best of 1m 57.8 seconds.

Akersloot returned to Holland, where he actually enjoyed quite a long career as a noteworthy factory-supported Ford Escort racer, and Bill was casting around for a driver. In Blydenstein's words: "It was difficult enough just to keep your head above water financially in a rapidly expanding conversion business: I had seen far too many business ventures go bust because *le patron* went motor racing. I decided I wanted to hire a dog, rather than bark myself".

According to Blydenstein Marshall was the obvious candidate. A test day was laid on early in the autumn of 1967 and Don Hagger was again part of the timing routine to make sure "... that young Marshall really did have the makings of a good Viva driver".

Gerry had been driving mainly a diet of respectably powered Lotus Elans and TVRs immediately prior to the test, with the result that, in Bill's words: "He lost those vital few mph on the exit to Russell: any gain in speed out of this corner added on all the way up the pits straight, could make a difference of well over a second a lap". On a good day the Vauxhall gave 95bhp, and must have weighed in at close to the big TVR's figures so it was not surprising that it took a little time for Marshall to adapt to this comparatively underpowered Vauxhall. Once he had seen what Bill was doing it took him three laps to equal the expected time so that there was no point in trying to point out any errors, Gerry was firmly in the driving seat. As Bill freely acknowledges today, and having tried it myself I can add my agreement, it's all very well saying that you can manage the same lap time as 55

I still say the trailer needs painting. Relaxing with a pot in our successful 1972 attack on the Forward Trust Championship.

Gerry Marshall. The really significant part of his armoury as a driver is his *racing* ability. Show him another competitor in front and he will worry at him in just the same way as the legendary British bulldog. This applies especially to the entry of corners in saloon car events, and was to lead to accusations of pushing, even when Marshall was plainly not guilty: he was and is not a saint, but his skill in shadowing a rival without touching belongs in the premier league of motor racing.

Blydenstein was not just some affable buffer who thought Gerry might do a good job. He had raced with a wide variety of saloons, including a spell in the factory-backed Mini-Cooper outfit when the really skilled Minibrick exponents were part of their efforts. By coincidence Blydenstein won the first ever BARC Cibie Saloon Car Championship in 1960: ten years later Marshall was also to take the BARC title, but this time Billy's Borgward Isabella TS had been transformed into a Viva GT. Before Marshall was able to race the car, Blydenstein gave the Vauxhall Viva its debut in this type of competition. Following a few sprinting and hillclimbing outings, Blydenstein ventured out in the Viva's first race, reported by the weeklies on April 13 1967. Again the track was Snetterton, this time the event was organised by Romford Enthusiasts A.C. Blydenstein was ninth overall.

Marshall and the Blydenstein Viva crossed paths again, later in 1967, when Gerry set a new class record in an E-type Jaguar at Woburn . Blydenstein was at the same hillclimb in the Viva. We were prepared for Marshall's appearance on the track with the Viva by an unsigned piece in *Motoring News* (probably written by present-day *World of Sport* commentator Andrew Marriott) that said: "Blydenstein will continue to race the S&K Viva with Gerry Marshall as driver". In *Autosport's* November 1967 columns they had a prophet who forecast that Gerry's impending appearance in the Romford District M.C.'s Brands Hatch meeting would offer: "Marshall, aged 25 years ... renowned for his tyre-smoking sideways attitudes in Minis and TVRs should be good value for money in this Viva!"

Our first time at Mallory with the Firenza in its original form. You can see we didn't know much about aerodynamics then: not even a front spoiler to our name. *Courtesy Colin Taylor*

The race itself was reported vividly in both magazines, detailing Gerry's eighth overall in the Viva for the Swiftsure Challenge. Marshall did well to finish at all: "... Bill Reiter from New York spun his Mini-Cooper in front of Gerry Marshall in the S&K Viva - the cars touched, but there was little damage and both continued to finish eighth and ninth". The race was headed by a pair of 1.8 Ford Anglia TCs: Roger Taylor, son of a Ford director, won and Tony Lanfranchi placed a 1-litre Fraser Imp third.

All concerned were really looking forward to the sohc 2-litre engine for the HB Viva (the ill-starred Viva GT), but what of the team that was built up behind Gerry? A team that was to provide everything from softly tuned road cars - which were also raced and sprinted in cases of crisis, occasionally by the staff - up to the beastly virtues of the V8 Ventora *Big Bertha* and Firenza-shelled *Baby Bertha,* also with that 5-litre Repco V8.

The personalities divide naturally into Vauxhall personnel, and those who surrounded Blydenstein.

The first step was to move into Shepreth railway station, the present Blydenstein /DTV headquarters. This was quite an occasion. Vauxhall people, like Jeremy Lawrence, joining those from Coburn Improvements (Billy's counterparts on the rally side for years until 1976) and Blydenstein for an official press 'do'. I remember the workshops were exceptionally smart, just as the cars always were, though everyone swears that DTV had to operate on a lot less money than any of their rivals. Gerry was in fine form and the whole 'do' emphasised what a professional little team was being built in this unlikely setting.

The Blydenstein team were at Shepreth by Summer 1969, by which time the Viva had taken its first outright win, in 2-litre form at Lydden Hill, July 20, 1968. *The* secret ingredient in both Marshall's Vauxhall success, and DTV's subsequent rally impact was added: Gerry Johnstone. The other Gerry arrived in October 1968, fresh from a job that was intended to be about writing service manuals for Vauxhall.

Both Blydenstein and Johnstone himself took a gamble in getting together. Gerry Johnstone told me: "Bill said there were no guarantees that S&K would continue. They needed some results, or that would be that. I had originally gone along to Blydenstein's to sort out another competition engine problem of my own. I remember Marshall was stamping his feet having failed to complete a lap without engine trouble and I sort of got involved: it finished up with me being offered a job!

"When I arrived Bill had a few blokes working for him on the cylinder head mods and two of them were spending evenings and afternoons looking after the racer. So, I was the first full-time racing mechanic. The first job I can remember was putting the GT2 camshaft in: that was worth 125bhp when paired up with the four-into-one exhaust manifold and a pair of 45 DCOEs. Nowadays we sell the same cam for ordinary road use.

"The first outing I can remember was to a Woburn hillclimb, and that's where I first got to know Gerry - though, like everyone else, I had heard about him, of course. That meeting saw us up against Alan Brodie's Viva V8 Chevrolet. At first I just thought they were all loonies, not worth taking seriously. Then I decided Gerry was quicker and braver than anyone else at the meeting, and that was a turning point.

"Not long after that I was looking after him at Lydden. There was no oil pressure after practice - during which he had the second fastest time - and I had to change the oil pump. Because I didn't panic, I think he thought I didn't care. Once that was sorted out we were just about inseparable for years". Marshall confirms that he did have strong doubts about Gerry Johnstone's suitability, when he had to show the new recruit through the elementary competition procedure. "When he had seen scrutineering once he got the idea fast enough", Gerry commented. "It was hard to know what Johnstone was thinking, but that he was thinking, and thinking usefully, was obvious from the car's progress", Marshall concluded.

Looking at an old picture of Johnstone it's almost impossible to recognise him as the same man as today's self-assured DTV team manager within the new Shepreth extension. There was a villainous Mexican bandit's mustache and hair slicked back in a style guaranteed to make the most fanatical Teddy Boy envious. There was and is nothing boastful about his speech though. Long pauses characterise his style, for Johnstone examines all the possibilities before replying and it was this quality, above all others, that set him apart from the crowd in Billy Blydenstein's estimation. He will simply stand and look at a mechanical problem for twenty minutes without uttering a word: when he does speak there's nearly always a practical solution proffered.

Gerry Johnstone was able to recreate for me the atmosphere of preparing for a club meeting with Marshall in the early seventies and later sixties so that I felt I was there. "I made the effort to try and get the car ready by Friday lunchtime to leave the Royston area. I would head off toward the M1 in the Bedford CA Van, calling at St. Albans for the Marshall man. He didn't have any money at all then, so I used to collect him up for the weekend. We'd be up and off for the racing weekend break, him as nervous as hell as a passenger, braking like hell into all the roundabouts! I'd tell him 'I'll drive this bit, yours comes later ...'.

"From a job point of view we started off with engine problem after engine problem, especially the head gasket. It became routine to change one before the meeting, and before the race, following practice! Gerry used to ask if he could help and I told him he certainly could - by keeping out of the effing way!

"It was definitely a seven day a week job in 1968, and it stayed that way until I switched over to the rallying side - now that's just the same. Except for one thing: I used to work on my own through Friday night, and usually through Saturday and the evening of that day as well. I'll tell you, it got really scary wondering what I'd do if the car fell off the jacks and trapped me. As it was, there was always the need to go and find somebody to help you load the car up when it was ready, so you knew you were on your own.

"I always knew one thing though: if you did your bit, he'd do the rest". As the man whose knowledge of Marshall as driver must be unrivalled I asked Johnstone for his assessment of his driver's abilities. A characteristic long pause before he replied: "As a driver he's far above club level in Britain. But he falls short of being a full international long distance driver. That is not because of his ability behind the wheel - and I reckon these long distance saloon car drivers are only a step down from F1 - but because he does not quite fit the mould. He will always say what he means ... there's no question of smooth talk: he'll say 'this is the blankity blank way things will be', and that's exactly the way they have to be!

"On the development side he was very useful indeed in the early days. Gerry knew if you had ± 2bhp. If he said it wasn't as good, or that the jet settings or cam profile were not right, you could take it that he *knew*. He wouldn't rate as a brilliant man on suspension. Obviously he understood neutral, under or oversteer but how you cured it was up to you, the mechanic. He would soon tell you if the car was better or worse. Just one thing he couldn't tolerate ... and that was understeer.

Following in Gerry Johnstone's shoes as Gerry's personal mechanics were Dick Waldock and Geoff Hall. Both joined within weeks of each other in 1970, when the Viva GT was going through an intensive development programme and both stuck to Marshall through thick and thin. They could always be found beavering away in some corner of the paddock, whatever the weather, and whatever the distraction offered by any of Gerry's friends. As a source of information they were both pleasant and accurate, which was no mean achievement when you remember the controversy that often surrounded championship club meetings.There might be a diplomatic silence when you asked for the facts, but generally they not only kept up Bill and the team's amazingly high standard of car presentation (little to do with money, more of time and attitude) but also found the often-needed self-control to keep a civil reply handy for the most inane enquiries.

Geoff Hall had been promoted to workshop foreman by 1978 while Dick Waldock was working on another tarmac car - a sort of *formule libre* Chevette *tubolare* (occasioned by its tubular framework) for hillclimbing when I researched this book. Either of them could have told me the following story, it just so happens it was Dick ... .

The account is a mechanic's eye view of Gerry's greatest international triumph, one that established yet again that he was a man of unusual courage and skill, beyond the bounds of scratching round Brands Hatch on a winter's day.

"Our proudest moment came in 1977, and even when it was happening I had a feeling we might be stopping racing that year. We built a new Magnum 2300 and I mean brand new, never turned a wheel in anger, or been sat in by Marshall until practice. It was what I would call a down-the-line Group 1 1/2 car in every detail, including the suspension mounting points. We had seen trouble before at Spa over the scrutineering for the British cars, and we didn't want any bother.

"The engine was built up the other end [of Shepreth's workshops-J.W.] , but Geoff did all the other Group 1s so I know they normally gave between 180 and a best of 188bhp. This one was detuned to 170bhp.

"We finished the car at twelve o'clock on the Wednesday before the event. We caught the two o'clock boat from Felixstowe (Gerry's co-driver, Australian Peter Brock doing the 1 1/4 hour drive to the ferry): we made Pete drive because we were both knackered, having worked all the week and the evening before.

"From Zeebrugge we went to Antwerp for the night, driving down to Spa on Thursday. We left the car and trailer at Malmedy and found our hotel. I can't remember the name, but it was the best in the area. That night you could say we had a drink, or that we were pissed as parrots, it's all the same after that much work.

"In the morning we went through the usual Spa procedure, driving the car down to the town for scrutineering in the park. It's a nice touch that, driving the competition car on the road. We had no problems at all at scrutineering, so we went back to the circuit ready to practise.

Factory visits were a part of my Vauxhall driving life - I can't understand why they didn't let us drive them. I always wanted to try a 12-wheel drift! *Courtesy Vauxhall Motors.*

"Sounds easy, doesn't it? At Spa there's nearly eight-hours of practice, covering a night session as well as daylight. The race starts on Saturday afternoon, so you've got to get the car right on Friday.

"We didn't have any trouble at all with the car, but there were various things to remember. Vic Hylens looked after our fuelling arrangements, and I remember the car did 6400/6500rpm in top on a 3.4:1 axle [around 140mph, at a guess - J.W.] and a five-speed gearbox.

"After practice we went back to our Vauxhall dealer at Malmedy and spent four hours checking over the car. That means every nut and bolt, then check each other's work to see that everything is right. You never want things falling off a racing car - but you especially don't want it to happen at Spa!

"You could say we had a drink that night, or that we were pissed as parrots etc. We had all the drivers at the hotel and one of Brock's Australian friends kept calling Gerry 'The Whale': it was a very posh hotel ... I don't know what they made of it all. Probably just shrugged their shoulders and thought we were mad English buggers.

"It was bloody cold in the mornings, you know? Anyway this mad Australian friend of Brock's also took to wearing Bermuda shorts. I think it was his way of protesting about all those smart GM people!

"On the Saturday we were at the circuit by nine or so. We occupied the time up to the three o'clock start laying out fuelling stuff, our tools and checking the car over again. Then there were thirty-six wheels and tyres to arrange, besides carrying on worrying about the car.

"We were at the track for about thirty-six hours in all. That means things seem to blur together, particularly when the celebrations are straight afterwards with no sleep and

Startling picture of an Elan being attacked by fast-moving Armco. I drive Victor Raysbrook's VRM Elan at Thruxton, one of many races where we started from pole but failed to finish. *Courtesy J. St. J. Bloxham.*

Testing with the Mathwall prepared BMW 3.0Si at Brands in 1973: the clash with my Vauxhall driving was too strong, so I had to stop driving after one race. *Courtesy Chris Todd.*

precious little food. Those were our celebrations I'm talking about, the official 'do' comes later.

"The big difference from our point of view is the long four-minute lap. You know the car should be around 4 minutes 34 seconds [the consistency with which Marshall and Brock matched each other was one of the key ingredients in their success - J.W.] and you start to panic if they're around the 5 minute mark, not realising that it could be wet on the other side of the track.

"We did have some problems in the race. The starter motor stopped working after five-hours or so - and they insist you have the bonnet down when you're starting the car there. We lost a place or so while we scrabbled round trying to find the bother. Once he got under the dashboard Geoff found it pretty quick: the wiring harness had parted.

"I think we got second place back because of the tyres. We were taking 10-seconds a lap off Vic's Magnum blokes in the dry, then we found we were *losing* 10-seconds a lap on them in the wet. That really means we were losing 20-seconds a lap. The Michelin bloke was very decent and literally gave us a set of TB 15s after we'd found out what fabulous tyres they were in the wet. We did one tyre change in the early morning light, leaving two Dunlop slicks on the front, and two Michelins on the back, to cope with a track that was drying out. Old Brockie reckoned it handled better like that! Gerry had the full set of slicks back on though".

In fact Brock did have an off against the Armco as well, but that didn't need any rectification on the spot. For Dick Waldock, grimy, red-eyed but proudly watching 'his' car going to second overall (and leading Vauxhall to the prestigious *Coupe du Roi* team prize) several memories clutter the finish. "Vic counted off every lap of the race and I sat on a chair only to fall off sound asleep. So I watched to the end, when the crowds carried us across to the car. It was a marvellous feeling: there was old Marshall and Brock, standing on the roof with the champers.

"After we'd packed everything up and gone six miles for the trailer, we had a bit of a change at the hotel. We got as pissed as pooftahs. Like Marshall, I'm strictly teetotal and it was the worst I've been: must have been the lack of food and sleep. By comparison, the prizegiving in the evening was very quiet: I think we'd all got hangovers!"

Ask Dick Waldock what he thinks of the man whose car he tended for so many years and you gain a swift appraisal. "My honest opinion is, in a big car he's unbeatable. There he can use the power to get out of trouble because his reactions are so good. He was definitely the greatest big saloon car driver in Britain when we were looking after him. We did con him a couple of times - not changing springs when he asked us to, that kind of thing, but I think we understood him well enough to do that.

"As a Group 1 driver he must have been pretty good too, because he always matched the times of others". Dick says it all rather sadly in the past, though Marshall was out and winning in Group 1 saloons the weekend following our talk, because Dick is talking purely about DTV.

"As a bloke he really had a heart of gold: dead soft in the middle. Not an over-generous man, but if anyone's in trouble he'll help them. He's a good business man though and not many would get anything from him there. We understand him ... "

The Vauxhall
decade

Part 1: The Vivas

"I can remember I made a fair start, bearing in mind the thing hadn't got *that* much power, but going round Bottom Bend this American idiot spun a Mini in front of me. Instead of spinning and staying out of the way, he did a reverse spin and came back right in front of me. I scraped the side of the car, and I was furious, having a series of words with him afterwards. I thought, here we are, my first race for Bill, and the car's got damaged already!" With those words Gerry Marshall recalls his racing debut with the Viva on November 12 1967, or the first time the Marshall/S&K Viva 1258 combination had appeared so far as the public was concerned. At that stage, Gerry perfectly summed up his feelings about the new partnership in an article he wrote for *Motor* many years later: "The car was very uncompetitive, being some 20bhp or so down on the equivalent Cooper 'S' and a lot heavier. But the preparation, handling and friendly team spirit was enough inducement to make me stay. Anyway, no one else wanted me!"

In fact, Marshall had done just what was required, breaking up the increasing monotony of a Ford or Mini diet that was offered to race-goers of the era and showing that there was definite potential even with only 1.3-litres to propel the comparatively large Viva HB shell.

How things were to change in that decade for these Vauxhall pioneers! Starting with barely 80bhp the team were to explore almost every cubic capacity between 2 and 2.6-litres with the subsequent Vauxhall single overhead-camshaft unit in the Viva. Some strange capacities were tried in the famous Thames TV Firenza, later dubbed *Old Nail*, but that settled upon 2.3-litres and over 240bhp, enough for Marshall to score sixty-three wins including class victories in this car alone, and capture a collection of Club Racing titles, including the 1972 Forward Trust Championship. When the latterly 16-valve, twin-cam Firenza made way for the V8s, Marshall and Dealer Team Vauxhall began to dominate club racing in a manner that would have been unthinkable to the onlookers first surveying that neat white and orange S&K Viva in the Paddock at Brands in 1967. First there was the beautiful but treacherous Ventora V8. Dubbed *Big Bertha* it " ... won all the races it finished", in Gerry's words, meaning that it won three of the six races it was entered in. That was *Big Bertha*, but the peak of their domination was to come with *Baby Bertha*, a Firenza-based special saloon that formed, in Marshall's masterful hands, an unbeatable combination in British and Irish races catering for what were unattractively-labelled Superloon races. By 1975 Marshall could appear against all the major opposition assembled to do battle in a supporting event to the British Grand Prix at Silverstone, demoralising that opposition by pulling out an enormous lead on the *first* lap, pushing the lap record to 110.10mph and winning by an enormous (38-second) margin. The pattern continued on until 1977, *Baby Bertha* and Marshall scoring twenty-nine victories, grasping lap records on *every* circuit at which they appeared. Marshall also drove an incredible number of Group 1, or Production Saloon events in Vauxhall Magnums, or Firenzas as the original coupes were known, and took innumerable class victories (even some brilliant outright wins when it was wet) to add to the grand total of one hundred and twenty-three outright victories scored by Marshall in ten years Vauxhall motoring. When it came to an end, at the close of 1977, Marshall could have said that he had brought it on himself ... he had simply been too successful. He had established Vauxhall as a credible marque, one that could appear in all sorts of competition with honour once more, no longer a laughing stock amongst the Leyland or Ford hordes.

He even brought on a number of drivers who continued to drive with success in Vauxhalls and were too successful there for comfort as well. The promising Jeff Allam came to prominence for the very reason that he was so successful in first harrying the original master, and then actually beating him once. It was the end of an era, the Magnum/Firenza promotion was no longer needed and international rallying became *the* priority at Shepreth. A quite beautiful 8.1-litre Vauxhall Cavalier mock-up was created to study the possibilities for special saloon car racing after *Baby Bertha's* sale, but it was felt by Vauxhall, who created this embryonic successor in association with DTV at their Luton base, that the prestige left in British racing was not sufficient to justify going ahead with the Cavalier project ... Gerry had simply been too successful in demolishing any opposition.

All that success was a far cry from 1967 though. After that initial outing there were more forays into sprints and a couple of club races at Lydden Hill. It was one of the latter, a televised event held right at the end of the year on Boxing Day 1967, that both Bill Blydenstein and Gerry particularly recall. Blydenstein simply says today: "It was the chance of a lifetime. We could have won our first televised event one and a half years before we actually did".

By this time the 1258 was reckoned to be giving 95bhp (about 15 more than when the project began) and the car was going well in practice at Lydden as Gerry recalls: "It was a bit damp, and we would certainly have won the race, but the diff, which was the *bête noire*, of this Viva, had the pinion bearing seize and we hadn't got a spare. We would have won because the guy in the Mini, who was slower than us, went on to win the race. It was just one of those things ... "

Marshall went on to say: "I also drove the car virtually with one hand because I had fallen through a window at home. I was stepping over the kiddy-gate partitioning off the rooms, when I slipped with a bound volume of *Autosport* in my hand, saved the *Autosport* and put my hand through the plate glass window on the door. I cut the hand pretty badly, and I still have no feeling in the thumb. I drove the car about four days later, effectively one-handed, but the 1258 was so light you could do that".

On the personal side 1967 for Marshall was: " ... the year of change. A year of very great uncertainties. I had one baby and there was obviously going to be another and a mortgage and no money! A year of some frustrations. Since 1966 Carol and I had been living at Chiswell Green Lane, St. Albans, three-hundred yards from the Three Hammers pub and up a nice little quiet lane. We had a cottage up there, flanked on one side by John Pope's farm and on the other by Derrick Brunt's farm. There's two people I managed to corrupt into motor sport at a later date!

"A glassfibre business which I began took a long time to get off the ground and I started trading. In fact in 1968 we wound up Gerry Marshall Ltd., which was that glassfibre concern. I was then on my own, I didn't need the overheads of these other people, or the aggravations".

Subsequently Gerry and Tony Lanfranchi formed an unofficial liaison using the money Lanfranchi gained from his Alan Fraser Racing Team retainer and Gerry's expertise to travel all over the country, making what Gerry described as: " ... a fairish living".

This went on until 1969, when Lanfranchi, " ... had his nasty accident on the road, on the way back from Silverstone. He 'fell off the road in a fit of alcoholic remorse', as Les Leston described it on television". The Marshall-Lanfranchi relationship also extended to Gerry filling in with some motor racing tuition work at Motor Racing Stables, Brands Hatch where Tony was, and still is, the Chief Instructor. That led to a short-lived single-seater involvement. That Gerry ever really got his trading career off the ground on his own was partially due to a £500 initial loan from John Wingfield, the two destined for a much closer business relationship a few years later, though the Marshall-Wingfield showrooms were not officially opened until 1972. Meanwhile, back on the track, the 1.3-litre Viva was developed further but with such a large body and such a comparatively small pushrod engine it was hard work even to score thirds and fourths in the class while racing. In sprints and hillclimbs things were a little better. A typical example was a sortie out to the annual Cambridge University Snetterton Sprint in February 1968, where Gerry and Bill shared the car while Martin Ridehalgh's Cooper 'S' won the class ahead of them. What they were waiting for was the new 2-litre engine which was to be slotted into the Viva to provide, along with some originally ill-conceived garishness (like four exhausts, and a good acre of matt black paint front and back), the Viva GT.

Marshall went along to see the new Viva at Vauxhall's Chaul End proving ground. Then in March 1968 " ... about a week after the announcement of the Viva GT, I went and did the Woburn Hillclimb, so I must have been the first person ever to compete with the Vauxhall overhead cam engine".

The 1968 season was to see Blydenstein provide Gerry with very rapid development indeed. The 2-litre Viva GT made its race debut in June of that year, probably with no more than 125bhp. By the last December outing in the traditional Boxing Day meeting Bill and the newly recruited Gerry Johnstone (his first event was an October Woburn Hillclimb, not the one referred to above) had engineered Tecalemit fuel injection onto the car, a system which was to stay in use on *all* their four-cylinder engines until the Firenza was honourably retired in 1975. Initially the engine would have yielded about 160bhp. Not only did the team provide an extra 60bhp and a lot more torque to pull the Viva along in 1968, they also provided Gerry with a lot of racing (seventeen events and two wins with the 2-litre) plus a few hillclimb and sprint outings. The Cambridge University Grand Slalom provided the first class win I can discover for a Viva in this type of event, in October 1968.

Tracing the first outright racing win for the Viva naturally involves the 2-litre Viva GT. The preliminary testing and some of the earliest races were carried out in a car that was modestly modified. The engine had a pair of 45DCOE Weber carburettors, there were closer ratios in the four-speed gearbox (a five-speed unit was not needed until the 16-valve Firenza arrived!), a limited slip differential, an all-round lowering of the suspension, which was mated to 1.5 degrees of negative-camber at the front. Minilite wheels and Goodyear racing tyres were used, but the brakes were almost standard, merely modified in respect of pads and linings. The car actually made its racing debut on June 9 1968 at Brands Hatch, but the press material was not released until July 1968. A short release on Shaw and Kilburn paper said the car would be: " ... initially entered in sprints, hillclimbs and club races, eventually it is hoped the car will compete in national and international events. The programme will be carried out for Shaw and Kilburn by Bill Blydenstein, who will be sharing the driving with Gerry Marshall".

The debut was not an auspicious occasion. Gerry's memories are: "Obviously the car attracted a lot of attention. Always being a shy, retiring, sort of person everybody kept coming and asking my opinion. Unfortunately, I gave it, as is my usual fashion! The reports of the car falling apart around me, though they might have been factual, were not strictly true. I remember Bill and Paul Harrington, the *Motoring News* reporter getting most unhappy about the whole thing. The car was quite demon: in those days we had *six-inch* Minilites, it was just untrue! It understeered and generally misbehaved as first-time out cars do, but it finished and that was the main thing".

Three wheels on my wagon. In 1973 I drove this Clan works demonstrator in the 6 Hours Relay: they went into liquidation within weeks ... *Courtesy John Gaisford.*

Having a skid in Alan Foster's Marina 1.8 at Silverstone. I think it's fair to say this was a unique experience, but in what sense?

Rare photo of intact rally car ... it didn't stay like that for long, which is why Rodney Spokes naturally looks apprehensive as we set off in my ex-Group 1 racing Magnum on a 1973 event. I ended up in Chesterfield Infirmary ...

The Firenza and I making ourselves unpopular at the BMW day. Brian 'Yogi' Muir drives the 1973 Alpina CSL in pursuit of Old Nail. He did win ... eventually! *Courtesy Motor.*

The Viva GT finished eighth overall, third in class on that debut performance. Just how fast the Ford Escort TC opposition of the time was can be gauged from the fact that Zakia Redjep managed a 58.6 second lap of the Brands Club Circuit on the way to winning the class, while Gerry's best in the Vauxhall was 62.4 seconds. The Paul Harrington report in question contained phrases about the Viva GT's debut such as: "... started to fall apart around him ... nevertheless Gerry had the admiration of everybody for his ability to save both the car and himself on the numerous occasions it threatened no good". This provoked a letter from the normally placid Bill Blydenstein pointing out what the car had achieved on its debut, Harrington replying with a published letter that showed how many people felt about the Vauxhall project at the time. The relevant remarks included: "The Viva Special makes a welcome break from the tedium of Ford and BMC. Excellent turnout and Gerry Marshall's fiery, but skilful, driving must always be a hit with the crowds. A win cannot be far away". Prophetic words indeed.

The truth of that prophesy was emphasised very quickly, for by the end of July the car had that victory. Gerry recalls the events of the next two racing weekends after that contentious debut: "The second race was again at Brands. This time on the mini-circuit which is never used today; people wouldn't believe it now. The track was the same as the Club Circuit but cut out the whole of the Clearways section, so you dived back up a sort of pit road to link Bottom to Top straight: I can't remember where they ever found room to put the finish!

"We managed second in that mini Brands and the third race we won. It was very good and showed constant improvement. We led from start to finish and it was very pleasing for us and for Vauxhall". That performance on the 'horrendous' mini Brands circuit was on July 14 and had *Motoring News* man Harrington eulogising on how the greatly revised Vauxhall showed signs of becoming: " ... a first class racer, particularly in the hands of such a fire-and-brimstone character as Gerry".

That first win with the Vauxhall came on July 20, at Lydden Hill, Kent, the tiny, twisting circuit better known for rallycross these days (especially of the international kind since it is virtually the first stop after Dover). *Motoring News* for July 24 showed how pleased they thought the team were: "Billy Blydenstein couldn't have been more chuffed if he'd found caviare in a cornflake packet", they wrote. The opposition was not too severe in this event, but it is interesting to note that the win took 10 minutes 45.6 seconds, an average 66.91mph, and that the fastest lap Gerry did was 52.6 seconds (68.44mph).

Their next event was during August and that was notable, as Gerry explains: "We did the Six Hour Race at Silverstone. In those days, and today for that matter, the name Jack Brabham was a name to be reckoned with. It was a very big name in Vauxhalls too, because of the old Brabham-Vivas. Brian Muir, who is not only an ace pedaller and a good friend of mine today, was also the number one mechanic at Brabhams on the conversion side. Obviously Jack Brabham's name had a lot more mystique attached to it than - with respect - did Bill Blydenstein's. Brabhams were trying to do a Brabham-Viva version of the GT. They turned up with their car with Webers all over it, racing tyres and a close-ratio box, everything.

"It was a confrontation between the Brabham and the Blydenstein offerings, in front of the public as well. Our car, with me driving, was faster than their's with Muir at the wheel. Whether we had done more development, or just done our development a bit better than them, I don't know - I do remember that we were running with a standard cam at the time for reliability and torque, and they had a high lift cam in. However ours was a touch quicker and honour was saved for Blydenstein. We never heard any more about a Brabham Viva GT". Both Vivas suffered mechanical ailments, but poor Muir also lost a wheel from his, so that was that: the team Viva was third, but had looked like winning for a while. Marshall had the compensation of a long dice with the man who had sold him those A35 parts in Luton, Jem Marsh in one of that gentleman's Marcos 1800s.

Brian Cutting (Escort V8) proves smoking can be harmful to your health: he was out on the next lap. Here the Firenza can be seen before the droop snoot was attached, but with the power bulge for the 16-valve engine, on its way to another win - this time at Thruxton in 1973.

The second win of the year was also at Lydden, but this time in September, and the event was confined to Vauxhalls, which at this stage of the game meant Marshall and his mount were 99 percent certain to win, especially as the race was held just after a thunderstorm. Again he led from start to finish, beating the supercharged car of the amiable Mike Davies (" ... rather scruffy, leaked a lot of oil ... and the car wasn't much better", quipped Gerry after trying the Davies machine for himself) by 13.2 seconds.

There were problems though as Gerry recalls "Deciding the specification was difficult. Nobody had used this engine at all in competition. We were lacking enough good mechanics: Bill could design a camshaft and modify the head and so on, but the mechanics often didn't know what they were doing. We were developing as we were modifying, which is always very difficult. We had a lot of oil pressure troubles, mostly from the oil pump and the fact that, if you machined the main bearing to racing tolerances, the oil pump had not got the capacity to supply these larger tolerances. We finally got it right and I would say the engine is the most reliable in the world now".

The Viva was improving with every outing though. At Mallory Park in October there was a second overall and fourth was recorded at Lydden in the same month. This drew comments that he " ... played the thing like a pike ..." and "... used the steering wheel like a meat cleaver" in one contemporary account. Sprinting was still much in the car's development schedule and two such events at Snetterton and Silverstone took up time for the last week in October and the first in November, yielding the first CUAC class win referred to earlier, and a third in class at Silverstone. Then the *Motoring News* account referred to him as: " ... the somewhat subdued Gerry Marshall, still suffering from the club's beanfeast the night before, who wound his arms into a fair imitation of a love-knot as he twirled the wheel."

Then came six successive outings for the car around the Brands Hatch Club Circuit, stretching from November 15 to December's Boxing Day meeting. These resulted in three second overall placings for Gerry Marshall and a third for Tony Lanfranchi. Tony drove the car because: "I was getting myself up to my knees in mud driving the Coburn rallycross car at Lydden Hill. The only notable thing about that was I convinced myself once and for all that Coburn couldn't prepare a car and that rallycross was muddy!"

Didn't we all look younger! Gerry Johnstone, myself and Dick Waldock (right).

Gerry commented. The event itself was not a triumph for Gerry, in fact he got back to Brands Hatch in time to see Tony's performance in the Viva! However he did bring the results sheets back from Lydden and recalls that a barman prompted him to look how well a certain Nick Whiting had fared, Nick then being a Kentish whiz at the muddy sport. Gerry did beat him on that occasion, which he regards as the first of the Marshall *v* Whiting confrontations, though Nick sees things a bit differently, naturally enough.

Amongst those end of season Brands outings there was one very fraught affair of ten laps that contained a 1-minute penalty for his start, a collision with Martin Birrane's 4.7 Falcon V8 and a subsequent race-long panel-to-panel race with John Wales in the extraordinary *Berpop* - some 1650cc of surprisingly agile and aged machinery. That experience left him feeling, " ... a bit annoyed afterwards. I was beginning to learn that people don't take pressure at all well in club racing. When you started getting close to them, put the lights on them, they tended to fall off or get panicked".

The race after that produced fastest practice time against good opposition and the Vauxhall was all set for its third win of the season, two-seconds ahead of Ken Costello's 1.3 Mini-Cooper 'S', when the throttle cable broke. Gerry says: "This was a great shame, as Costello was the big man to beat in those days. It was a wet race and we had it in the bag".

The next weekend Gerry was out proving how vastly improved the Viva was, finishing second overall to Mike Crabtree's " ... properly prepared and driven", in Gerry's words, Escort Twin Cam. The feature of that outing was that Gerry spent seven of the ten laps humbling Nick Faure's ex-Vic Elford Porsche 911, which brought the Vauxhall driver to joke: "He had no right to be grovelling right at the back of the field with me!" It was during this two-day race meeting that Gerry borrowed the Davies Viva GT for practice, as his own car had a gearbox problem. From this time he recalls that Ken Davies was often a dicing compatriot, driving an immaculate Anglia Twin Cam with talent; the Shaw and Kilburn Viva GT Special also had a new nickname - "The 128bhp

Stuart Turner and others may have called us all sorts of names, but Roger Clark and I were happy enough with the first and second place finish on the 1974 Avon Motor Tour of Britain. *Courtesy Martin Holmes.*

Slap and Tickle Special!"

By the first meeting of December 1968 the Viva was improved enough to finish within a second of Crabtree's Escort at Brands. The highlight was the December 27 meeting (he always seems to wake up on Boxing Day; this event described as "Cold, clear and dry, in the best glassy-eyed tradition") when he took on the highly respected Roy Pierpoint in Bill Shaw's 4.7 Falcon V8, a car capable of winning at internationals. "Boxing Day was actually a big milestone in Vauxhall development. Bill had been working on race cams and fuel injection. The engines were giving prodigious power by our standards: 170 bhp was the figure bandied about by the men of the 'bob-and whistle brake', down at TJ! We thought we'd be so fast it'd be hard to catch your breath in the car. Alongside us on the grid for the front row was Pierpoint: we had a tremendous battle: he beat me, but I led him several times", Marshall remembers, adding: "The whole thing of driving the Viva was now very different. Where before I'd been getting maximum power at 5800-6000rpm, I was now having to use 7000rpm with no torque. In fact the lap times weren't any quicker, but it seemed it. Now we had a racing saloon car as opposed to a racing saloon with a modified engine: this meant we could do the thing properly and it would go bang at higher revs!

"The car that we had been using up to now was, in fact, the original 1258 Viva shell. It had been shunted at Snetterton hairpin by Han Akersloot, repaired as a shell and had become the original Viva GT. The 1258 S&K Viva Special was built from new, and was subsequently sold to Jeremy Lawrence. So the Viva GT had never been a new car to me: it was a crash rebuild, although it looked very smart. Gerry Johnstone was very enthusiastic then and we used to have 'a tweak of the week' literally every week. The car was very well turned out and its reliability was good, apart from a lot of head gasket problems in 1969. Bill and Gerry were working on head gasket design and, eventually, we licked it of course, but it took a long time as the compression ratio went up". That was Gerry's Vauxhall opinion at the beginning of a year that was to see him take in twenty-six races in the Viva

71

GTs, fighting a momentous season-long battle against George Whitehead's purple and purposeful 1860cc pushrod engined Anglia.

For some time though Gerry Johnstone and the boys at Shepreth had been working on a new car for Marshall and that was unveiled in May 1969, though it didn't race until June - when it had a 2-litre engine - then in late July the car finally appeared with the welded crankshaft 2.3-litre engine. It was a troubled year, but it yielded four outright wins, one of them before a TV audience of nine-million, so it was very important to the team. There were also four class wins, seven second overall placings, and a twenty-five lap contribution to the win recorded by the Viva team in that year's Six Hour Relay.

This was the year that plenty of rumours were circulating to the effect that Marshall would be seen in F5000, but while this hope progressively faded away, the Redex title became more of a reality. After three rounds he led the Anglia driver by two points and by May the score was twenty-two to the Vauxhall and sixteen to the Ford.

Good Friday was on April 4 that year and the Vauxhall team was up at Oulton Park to do battle in front of an estimated forty-thousand spectators drawn by the annual Gold Cup feature race, the TV cameras also covering the saloon car event. Gerry was fastest in practice and won by 0.4 seconds which made Vauxhall pretty happy. "The car ran perfectly and the whole performance was pretty good news", Marshall recalls, together with the ex-works registration number of the Lotus Cortina that was second, driven by Peter Jackson.

Most frightening incident of the year came in another Oulton Park event, but during the warming-up lap, Marshall was: " ... flying down to Knickerbrook, lifted off and braked. The throttle stuck fully open. So I had to concentrate on stopping it before I switched the ignition off: the plug leads had got stuck under the fuel injection cam and jammed it open. I got back to the pit and it had even turned the fan belt inside out". This was actually the first appearance of the new car and Gerry Johnstone did wire the plug leads out of the way, but the engine was obviously affected because it blew up in the race while Mr. Marshall was battling along in third place. Now Gerry reckons: "That actually cost us the championship for we had Whitehead beaten that day".

Best race of the year came with Marshall on pole position in the 2-litre engined Viva for the October Grand Prix circuit, BRDC Championship meeting at Silverstone. "Bob Torrie and Richard Longman were beside me, Longman in a Mini of course, and Bob Torrie driving that beautiful BRM twin cam-engined Escort. Just before we went into the marshalling area I had a puncture in the left front tyre. So they put another tyre on with a different compound, which made it understeer a bit and cost a second and a bit a lap. In the race I had a tremendous battle with Bob Torrie, Longman and Hugh Denton (another good friend of mine, also driving a 1300 Mini). I never did get down to my practice time (1 minute 47.4 seconds) because of the tyre problem. Bob just pipped me but we slipstreamed by each other for the fifteen laps of the race. I subsequently bought the Escort in 1971, which was the car in which Derrick Brunt debuted in racing and it subsequently went on to John Pope, so it stayed in the Marshall neighbourhood".

A riotous trip to Ireland for the Phoenix Park races in the autumn - " ... super party the night before the race, because after all there was going to be a party after the race, so Irish logic demanded there be one before as well. There was one mechanic who was quite upset at his driver commandeering his room for nefarious purposes with a young lady at one of those 'dos' but I can't imagine his annoyance was anything to do with our clean living team, or that the mechanic was upset because he wasn't getting any ... can I? Anyway, we were fastest in practice, but I had to read Vinny Moy his fortune after he knocked me off on the first corner of the race. I've never been back to Phoenix Park since to race, more's the pity. Super people and super hospitality", concluded Marshall with a reminiscent gleam in his eye.

The last round of the Redex Championship was at Brands Hatch, with George Whitehead already declared champion, though he had endured a very nasty Formula Ford accident late in the season. Held in early November the weather was pretty horrible and damp, but the Vauxhall team made the pleasant gesture of asking George to drive their 2-litre Viva GT in his first outing since the accident. Unfortunately a halfshaft failed and Whitehead did not finish the 10-lapper in which Gerry scored his final win of the year. Earlier the same day Gerry had taken a second place in the Viva, beaten by Peter Hawthorn's rapid Mini in the diabolical conditions, though it didn't really matter from a Redex Championship point of view as the series was already a foregone conclusion in Whitehead's favour, and the Mini would not affect Marshall's points tally.

The penultimate race of the year was Gerry's first visit to Thruxton for a televised affair. He made another of his demon starts and led the initial laps, but both Richard Longman's Mini and Martin Birrane's Falcon had passed him by the finish. However, Gerry fared much better than the Ford phalanx of names - Birrell, Craft and Brodie all went off in the opening lap! Looking at 1969 today Gerry says: "We were having problems with diffs, mainly in making them reliable. In fact I was running a locked-up differential in those days, which made the cars even more untidy and spectacular in appearance - which I possibly didn't need. It was a super-handling car though; I don't think I spun all year and I don't think we ever hit anything. It was a good, competitive year".

At the close of the season the Vauxhall's 2310cc had taken power from 160bhp at 6500 rpm to a quoted 200bhp nett.

The 1970 season saw Vauxhall reaching out through Bill Blydenstein for international honours. Their efforts were not very well rewarded but Marshall did get his first outing at a circuit that was to bring him even greater rewards, and that was the Spa-Francorchamps track in Belgium. That brought a fourth place in this international, a result they duplicated at Zolder. Technically speaking Blydenstein and Marshall took on an impossible task: they would continue their club racing programme but invade the world of International Group 2 with the Viva GT in 2-litre form. For this type of racing the Viva had to forego the lightweight glassfibre panels used in British club racing, and had to be below 2000cc to comply both with international homologation procedure and the requirements of the capacity class they were contesting. However, the club cars were to get considerably more reliable during the year as Blydenstein was able to gain access to some early pre-production, 2.3-litre sohc, crankshafts, which he enthusiastically described as: "The strongest cranks in the business: we never looked back from that point on".

Equipped with a 180-horsepower 2-litre engine, and their international Group 2 homologation forms, the Shepreth team set out on what was to be an expensive year. "We did not finish a race on the Brands Hatch Grand Prix circuit. I rolled it in the first race, the Race of Champions. I've forgotten the reason I rolled it now ... perhaps it was just ineptitude! Up at Dingle Dell it fell over at about 2mph literally, after I had spun. It was a gentle spin, but it clipped the kerb, and, oh so *slowly*, it toppled over. That was OK but the marshals then rolled the car up the right way, over the good side! I thought that was most unnecessary ... " A grin spread across Marshall's visage at the memory. A second appearance at Brands Hatch for the Grand Prix supporting event was no luckier. "I had a tremendous dice with John Bloomfield's Escort Twin Cam. He was quicker up the straights and I was a bit faster round the corners. On the last lap, last corner [Clearways], I tried a bit hard. The diff had been giving me trouble throughout the race, creaking and groaning. It finally locked up solid and I went into the bank backwards, which didn't enamour me to Bill at all".

Blydenstein looks back on that foray into the unaccustomed Group 2 scene with unusual mirth. That set of competitors was dominated at the front by Frank Gardner's 5-litre Boss Mustang and in Gerry's 1300-2000cc class by Escorts. The smaller Fords started

This RS2000 won the Mintex with Roger driving but failed testing with me at Bagshot (rolled!)... *Courtesy Martin Holmes.*

Roger never has liked tarmac! On the Tour of Britain 1974, Roger Clark's works RS2000 leads my car at Cadwell Park. We finished about this far apart after racing like this at virtually every British circuit: neither car was scratched! *Courtesy Colin Taylor.*

This Avenger cost me my no claims bonus! The ex-Slade Avenger leads Tony Shaw's Capri through the Thruxton chicane: a week later it was written-off at Brands Hatch by a Camaro that was controlling its driver, rather than vice-versa! *Courtesy J. St. J. Bloxham.*

This is NOT a rallycross picture! Barrie Williams and I scramble for the line at Thruxton in the 1974 Firenza race. *Courtesy Colin Taylor.*

off with 170 to 180-horsepower Twin Cam engines, but during the season the 16-valve Cosworth BDA motor arrived, making outputs of 200bhp and more possible. Blydenstein recalls the accidents of course but of the earlier one at Dingle Dell he also records: "Brand X had been trying to get Gerry to use one of their safety harnesses. So he had a brand new set of belts in the car, but he just couldn't get them undone: can you imagine it, eighteen stone of Marshall trying to get loose".

In the effort to keep up with the Escorts, Blydenstein recalls: "Our second biggest ever blow up!" At the time they were practising the still-immaculate Shaw and Kilburn-backed Viva for the Snetterton round of this British RAC Group 2 Championship. As Bill says today: "Gerry turned in a fabulous practice performance. He was only half a second or so adrift on the fastest Broadspeed Escorts. He came in and complained of a vibration and that the oil pressure had dropped. We sent him back out again to try something else. Marshall got to Sear and was changing gear when BANG!, there were bits all over the road. Even the gearbox and the axle were damaged. When we got the engine back to the workshops we discovered it was literally the sump that was holding it together: we removed two bolts and the whole unit disintegrated into a thousand pieces!"

At that time the finances of the team cannot have allowed any of them to see the incident with the quite surprising candour and humour that is evident now. Other teams appeared to be on even rockier ground though. After a club-racing dice with Colin Hawker's SuperSpeed Escort V6 ("A lovely crisp engine note", as Gerry recalls) at Silverstone, SuperSpeed boss John Young phoned Blydenstein to ask if the Vauxhall team would pay for a damaged windscreen suffered during the dice. "*Strange* people", mused Mr. Marshall at that recollection. "I don't think Colin and I talked for three years after that. He really thought I'd thrown stones at him deliberately".

Although the year did offer five outright wins and two class victories the first taste of overseas recognition was not for a win. The month was May and Gerry had travelled to the Belgian side of the Ardennes Forest to compete in a saloon car race of sprint duration by the standards of the circuit - the eight miles per lap Spa-Francorchamps road course, which is also the host circuit for the July 24 Hour event. Asked to name his favourite circuit in a recent interview Gerry said: "Spa goes at the top of the international list, without question. I always think Spa is something else. The driving technique is quite different, it's quite possible to be gentle on a car there. For me the best section is downhill through Burnenville and on to Malmedy. I used to like Malmedy itself, but now they have a chicane so I prefer Stavelot crossing. Masta (Kink) has always been flat-out in Vauxhalls, so the other bits are more interesting. I think the Vauxhall is going quicker into Burnenville than on the main straight!"

For that race in 1970 the practice session was wet and Marshall made a real impression in the Group 2 Viva, taking second place on the grid and lining up alongside Jacky Ickx, then driving a V8 Mustang borrowed from Dennis Leach the West Country garageman. Unfortunately the race was dry and Marshall counted himself fortunate to extract enough speed from his 2-litre mount to hold on to fourth position on a circuit where cornering speeds well above the Vauxhall's maximum are routine. That was not the end of it though for in the prestigious British monthly magazine *MOTOR SPORT* the legendary Denis Jenkinson (D.S.J.) was reflecting on what was to be the last Belgian Grand Prix. Famous for his views of motor racing safety and circuits, D.S.J. included the following paragraph in the issue of July 1970. "I am often told that we should listen to what the top drivers have to say as they are important to the world of motor racing. Personally, I think most of what they say is influenced and biased by their business sense, and that is nothing new, as you can see by reading things drivers said, or were reputed to have said, back in the 1930s and 1920s. I prefer to listen to the not-so-famous, who have no big business deals or managers to butter-up and be nice to. Earlier at Spa, during the 1000 kilometre sports-car meeting, there was a saloon car race and among all the continentals with BMWs and Alfa Romeos was a Vauxhall Viva giving as good as it was getting. It was driven by an English clubman, one Gerry Marshall, and he was really enjoying himself and saying that at long last he was discovering what motor racing was all about, having never experienced anything so marvellous as the Spa circuit".

Part II: Firenza - a star is born

The 1971 season was a very eventful one for our hero and the results started to arrive in a lump. At the end of the season *Autosport's* records showed that he had won *twenty-two races* outright, taken two more class victories and five lap records, three of them in Vauxhalls. For prestige he had his first outright title - Escort Mexico Challenge Champion 1971! It was ironic that it should be a Ford that provided his first major title, but as is proper whilst writing about these GM matters in this chapter, we have banished the account of that performance, along with other significant non-Vauxhall honours and amazing tales to a later chapter. You must read on, if only to see what he says about Jody Scheckter!

Meanwhile back in our Vauxhall world we find that 1971 also brought Gerry the Osram GEC class title (in the biggest capacity division), taken after scoring eight wins, and two second places, in the thirteen qualifying races. Considering that this was the year of Mick Hill and his Capri V8 Saloon Special, the combination that was the top-scoring one in the United Kingdom with thirty-one outright wins to its credit, Marshall's performance was extremely creditable, especially as there was also David Brodie's very rapid 2.1-litre Escort Twin Cam to contend with. The flamboyant Brodie's black car carried the slogan 'Run Baby Run' and was also credited with twenty wins, so it must have been hard for anyone else to get a look at a chequered flag in saloon car racing that year.

However there were two very significant events on the team front which affected all concerned, especially our Mr. Marshall. In January 1971 the principles behind the formation of Dealer Team Vauxhall were agreed at a meeting of the Vauxhall Dealer Council, London Region. In May 1971 a committee was formed to promote racing and rallying activities (still the responsibility of Chris Coburn and company at that stage) and that committee really controlled DTV. Alan Maidens of GN (Croydon) Ltd became Chairman and Lionel Altman, one of the key figures behind the appearance of the Shaw and Kilburn support that had carried the racing thus far, was appointed Secretary of DTV. Since 1975 Blydenstein has acted as Chairman of the committee, while Vauxhall are represented through their merchandising manager, Richard Angus. The other outside event that affected Gerry's Vauxhall racing life was the gradual introduction of the competition Firenza, the coupé version of the Viva being introduced to the public that year, which was just as well, since a sensational accident at Lydden Hill wiped out both club-racing Vivas in the hands of Mike Crabtree and Roger Bell! By the end of the year the Firenza held two of the three Vauxhall lap records which Gerry had established.

That year was also notable for the number of engine size permutations Blydenstein could make now that he had a sound crankshaft to work with. The 2.5-litre was rated at 214 bhp but, " ... although down on bhp it was very much up on torque and throttle response". Gerry noted in an article he wrote for *Motor* some years later. The other permutations were 2.2-litres, 2.3-litres, and 2.6-litres, but the 2.5-litre version of the sohc four was used until 1972 for the Firenza's original winning performances.

It was on September 9 that the Firenza, then painted steel-grey and blue and called the Thames TV Firenza, was handed over by Alan Maidens to Eamon Andrews. The accompanying press material claimed a maximum speed of 140mph and a sprint from rest to 100mph in thirteen seconds for the new mount. Meantime Marshall was doing very well in the club racing Vivas and was always faster in the Viva than in the new Firenza when they did back-to-back testing! On September 16 the Firenza 2.5 appeared in public at a race meeting for the first time, being practised for an Osram Championship round but not used as Gerry reverted to the Viva for the race. This a TV epic of twenty minutes which he won after a fabulous scrap with Martin Thomas (5.7 Chevrolet Camaro V8!)

Chap having a skid at Mallory Park one Sunday afternoon. A favourite picture of the Firenza ('Old Nail') in later beak-nose form with 16-valve engine. *Courtesy J. St. J. Bloxham.*

though the 'on-the-road-winner' was Mike Crabtree, his Escort performance penalised a minute for jumping the start. On Sunday, September 26, the Firenza did make its debut at the South Wales ex-airfield track of Llandow, winning both a saloon car and sports car race at this smaller club meeting, and establishing a new lap record.

October brought Marshall back to Lydden Hill, this time Firenza-mounted (Thames TV-sponsored for a BBC race! They had to mask the sponsorship though) and facing his faithful Vivas - loaned on a one-off basis to then *Motor* editor Roger Bell and the experienced Mike Crabtree, plus Marshall's pet *bête noire,* David Brodie in the big-engined Escort. To say the race was action-packed is the literal truth. On the first lap, first corner, Bell and Crabtree were involved in a wild *mêlée* that wrote-off both of the Vivas: they were never used by DTV again.

The drama was not over though, for as Marshall slowed at the completion of the lap to negotiate the debris left by the first corner carnage, Brodie was through and leading after skipping across the grass! Gerry was, " ... furious. In my opinion Brodie had over-taken me under very dangerous circumstances and the race should really have been stopped. There were cars all across the track". It took Marshall until lap eight to fight his way back to the front, despite the desperate manoeuvres performed by the black Ford to prevent the Vauxhall re-asserting itself. Talking about the incident in 1978 Marshall said: "It was a fair win. I had fastest lap and a new record (47.0 seconds/76.6mph). It also meant I *had* to run the Firenza, because I hadn't got anything else to run!

"With no choice of car left, I had to get used to going as quickly (if not quicker) in the new car and like it! The Firenza was a fairly vicious oversteerer at this time, the Viva having been noted for mild understeer. [I obviously wasn't paying attention. Marshall doing anything mildly, never mind understeering, seems as likely as an elevation to the priesthood - J.W.] This had us fooled for a bit as all weights, suspension and settings were identical to those on the Viva GT. The reason was that the Firenza shell is incredibly strong torsionally and we found that my previously used roll bars were unnecessary", Marshall added in an interesting aside.

The 2.6-litre engine, which was noted as having about 210bhp and the same figure

Jock Robertson (hands on hips) surveys the Snetterton breakers yard with his car underneath, driven by your truly! *Courtesy Stephen Jones.*

given as an approximate guide to the extraordinary torque, scored a fine win when installed for the second time on an outing to Mondello Park in Ireland, earlier that year. The entry list read like a *Who's Who?* of club saloon car racing and included both Hill's Capri and Brodie's Escort, plus the scorching little turbocharged Complan Mini of Alec Poole. The race turned into a three-way struggle between Hill, leading by half an inch over the Viva, which was in turn under seige from 'The Brode'. In fact Brodie retired after an accident and Gerry, " ... by dint of having a go, won. Fortunately the straight isn't very long there. I just drove as hard as I could the *whole* time". Blydenstein remembers this as a classic case of Gerry's constant pressure behind Hill as the key to this win, for the Capri V8 driver eventually had a spin and the Vauxhall was away to win what was regarded as *the* saloon confrontation of the day.

During 1971 we also saw the first hesitant steps towards a class of racing that is now the accepted basis for the majority of British events, production car racing. These first events were run on a handicap basis as organisers struggled to get to grips with a form of racing that brought many a tyre-squealing induced tear to the older observers' eyes. Tyre squeal? Everyone had almost forgotten it in the welter of highly modified saloons used at every level of British and European racing: giant slick tyres and sophisticated suspension systems had made the sound of tortured rubber instantly nostalgic. Naturally Gerry was involved and, as was often his practice in years before when sprinting or hillclimbing, he used his road car, a yellow 2-litre Firenza (EXE 685J) and drove it in such awesome style that it is thought some onlookers may still be picking bits of flayed, fried rubber (try saying that if you're Japanese) from their hair! That car was also used to complete his stint at the relay that year, the stereo acting as some solace for previous gasket troubles with the racer.

October 1971 marked another Marshall probe into his future. That was the date of his first column in a national motoring magazine, *Cars and Car Conversions*. The present editor of that publication, the incredibly brave Terry Grimwood, was chosen for his drinking stamina and general boy scout enthusiasm to try to drag this literary masterpiece from the master's lips every month. The combination of Terry's humour and Gerry's natural sauciness did prove too much for both the lawyers and then-editor Paul Davies (now DTV's public relations man) on occasion. As Grimwood once revealed, the biggest problem was: " ... remembering if I had got the copy out of him and which train I'd left it on". The Little House Club in London's West End had claimed another victim, usually leaving Marshall and Lanfranchi to " ... carry on supping", wondering why their journalistic companions were turning green or cluttering the place up by snoring on the floor.

To get those twenty-two outright wins in 1971 gives an idea of how busy Marshall must have been, but it wasn't all racing. Between his first outing (January 17) and his last (December 5, also at Brands Hatch) he attended thirty-two competitive events for Vauxhall alone, never mind the rounds of the Mexico Challenge. Truly a year-long effort, but 1972 looked busier with a new Castrol-backed series for Group 1 saloons containing fifteen rounds alone.

The close of the 1971 season saw a low point for Gerry though. Chasing Norman Abbott's radical Escort into Clearways at the Brands Hatch Boxing Day meeting, there was a collision between the back of the lurid pink Ford and the shadowing Firenza. The crowd in the stands, who were viewing the incident diagonally across the infield at least a quarter of a mile away, reacted with unprecedented scenes when Marshall arrived at the finish to collect his reward for winning. They booed and the RAC subsequently disqualified Gerry from the race-win, after a tribunal held at his own request. "We had a glassfibre front on the Firenza, but there was not a mark on it. The car went straight off to a racing car show stand, so there was no question of my having pushed off Abbott deliberately, as has been frequently alleged", was Marshall's comment on this incident some years later. At the time the pro-Marshall and pro-Abbott camps dominated club racing conversation and the letters columns of the sporting weeklies.

Despite the bad taste of the tribunal and a year dogged by accidents in Group 1, 1972 was one of his best seasons in racing. The 2.5-litre Firenza carried on with what Bill Blydenstein once described as: " ... the fastest tractor engine in racing" and pulverised the opposition in the Forward Trust Saloon Car Championship of that year. Altogether Gerry scored twenty-seven wins that year (seven of them class victories) which left him fourth in the annual *Autosport* table of club race winners. He also took two lap records in Group 1, and then two in club racing using three Group 1 Firenzas, which started at 2-litres and bred into Firenza 2300s by the end of the year; he also took his class in the new Castrol Group 1 Championship, which there was no chance of winning outright as his mate Lanfranchi was winning the cheapest class on each outing ... driving a Moskvich 412!

In between the hectic racing schedule Gerry had to fit in show appearances. At the start of the year it was the imaginative but ill-starred Showboat promotion on the Thames, the DTV Firenza being transported straight from that Townsend Thoresen ferry onto another boat leaving for Belgium and the Brussels Motor Show. This is how he recounted the journey to *Cars and Conversions* readers in the March 1972 issue.

"This was my second trip to Belgium within a week as I'd previously taken over my old Viva GT (risen from the Lydden ruins). Everything was smooth on the first trip, but this time I was beset with every drama in the book including a punctured trailer wheel on arrival at Ostend (no spare!), very much the wrong importation papers (like none!), and owing to European time being an hour behind us, all my contacts at General Motors having gone home to bye byes. Consequently - no reception committee!

"As me no parley any language at all, including English on this occasion, I was obviously a mentally disturbed item to be pitied. So ... somehow we were released on an unsuspecting Belgian populace with our one-sided trailer.

"Then I repaired to the nearest garage and jokingly asked for the puncture to be fixed. After various multi-lingual discussions we decided to put a tube into the tubeless tyre. Only snag was breaking the bead on the tyre. If you've ever tried to remove a wide-rim tubeless radial from a 10 inch wheel without proper equipment you'll know exactly what our problems were - it wouldn't come off no how!

"Eventually we managed by lodging a piece of wood on the top of the tyre and lowering the four-poster hydraulic garage lift, complete with car, onto the piece of wood to apply pressure. It worked!

"By the time I got to the show salon *tempus* had *fugited*. It was a bit like arriving at Earls Court for the Motor Show at 10 pm on the night before press day - complete with a car to go on a stand.

"So ... all the side-doors were bolted and barred and the only way in was the main entrance. Feeling rather like Cinderella I drove the whole *équipe* up the steps and into the main hall.

"The General Motors stand was in fact right over on the far side of the hall and with the help of two apparently inebriated Belgian Andy Capps I persuaded the whole ensemble to the stand. This took the best part of an hour because I had to drive over (literally) some stands. I eventually finished up on the Mercedes stand with the towing Firenza perched on its exhaust manifold - stuck fast.

"It took many hands to manhandle it off. All's well that ends well though, and eventually we got the racing Firenza onto the GM stand, alongside its older Viva sister. With my exhaust blowing merrily to all and sundry I went off to find a hotel for the night.

"Next day, when the show opened, nobody appeared to notice the tyre marks right across the carpet on the Merc stand ..." And that was just an excerpt from what was a typically adventurous trip!

In the first of the Group 1 races, held on a miserably misty day at Brands Hatch, Marshall's Firenza 2000 annexed pole position running on Gerry's then-traditional Goodyear racing covers. In the race Roger Bell's BMW 2002Tii proved too much to cope with - as it did until the bigger capacity Capris, BMWs and the Chevrolets appeared - but Gerry finished a good second overall. It was eventful all the way through the Group 1 season though, for at the Castrol Group 1 round held at Thruxton Gerry's Firenza was disqualified for being 40 thousandths of an inch overbored. "We'd won the class and the scrutineers picked our car at random to have a look at. I was standing about in the scrutineering bay and Andy Dawson (the rally driver, then with Chrysler Competitions) was doing his impression of *Jaws*, wittering away. I know Andy very well now and like him very much, but his attitude can get up your nose when it's your car he's nosing around! The scrutineers said they wanted the head off, to measure the valve sizes, so I said that while they were about it, why didn't they measure the engine size? I told them they would find it was straightforward 40 thou. oversize: Andy leapt on that straight away and pointed out you weren't allowed to overbore. I said we could, the car was homologated at 40 thou. oversize. They measured it - actually Andy had to show them how - and found, sure enough, it was 40 thou. oversize. It was very embarrassing because Vauxhall had *not* homologated that tolerance. The last thing DTV ever wanted to do was run an illegal car ... and it could have cost us the championship as well because we were stripped of the points, even though a tribunal found our action was unintentional".

A wet Oulton Park round of the same series provided more Vauxhall camp embarrassment as Tim Stock spun his Firenza at Lodge and was waiting, nose-first, when Gerry hove into view in his similar car on slicks ... crrunnch! In August/September things were a lot more serious, for the 2.3 with wider wheels generated a serious stress problem in the Firenza halfshafts. To the horror of the Brands Hatch crowd, Gerry lost a rear wheel first at Druids - when there was a fire and a very real risk of burning to death in the inverted car - and within a fortnight it had happened again on the same track, on the same lap with less dire results. Gerry was plucked from the car by brave BRSCC marshals in the first instance, but on the second occasion he just sat there the right way up. His curses were heard in Luton and, although there was no danger anticipated for hard road use, the production shaft diameter was increased by 1/16th inch.

Gerry's final Group 1 accident of the year came at Snetterton when the brakes locked   *81*

Pride of the BRDC - or who feels a right tit! From left to right, Gerry Marshall, Stirling Moss, Tony Lanfranchi, the real thing, Mike Wilds, Peter Gethin and Graham Hill. An annual dinner to remember. *Courtesy Gerry Stream.*

up going into the second corner on the first lap: even at that stage the contest had already lost some of their number in an aerobatics display at the first corner: Group 1 was like that! The Marshall Firenza rolled pretty vigorously. Almost as soon as it came to rest Gerry was out and running for the twin-engined Comanche aircraft that was to take him to Thruxton for a critical qualifying round of the Forward Trust Championship. He made it there alright, signatures from all the other drivers allowing him to do the race which was abandoned after four laps because of high wind and rain. He had done enough to ensure that title though, and, at their annual ball, the BARC recognised what had been a very hard but successful year for this well known Club member, awarding him the BARC President's Cup.

Together with Gerry's reputation, that of the Firenza club car was fast growing as a winning force. In its first year the Vauxhall, which was dubbed *Old Nail* as the seasons rolled by, won nine races. The following year, 1972, the Firenza took fifteen wins while 1973 saw the car credited with twenty-one victories and three lap records in Gerry's hands.

In 1973 technical progress took a leap forward, for the Firenza went over to a Lotus LV240 cylinder head in aluminium for the March 11, Formula 2 International meeting at Mallory Park. Because the injection trumpets sat higher in the chassis, a distinctive "phallic lump", in Gerry's words, was incorporated in the bonnet and the car sported a front spoiler: by the end of the year Vauxhall had introduced their 'Droop Snoot' Firenza and the competition car also featured that nose, together with a rear spoiler, wider rear Minilites and dry sump lubrication. The 2.3-litre capacity had come about in 1972 and utilised a great number of standard components, but the 16-valve unit initially had special pistons that brought the capacity to 2.2-litres for a few events. The car had some 230 bhp in this 16-valve form initially, but it was the increased high-speed torque that led

I hope Barrie Williams doesn't sit on my knee! *Courtesy Colin Taylor.*

to the final abandonment of the faithful four-speed gearbox with Blydenstein designed close-ratios, a five-speed ZF coming into use by October.

Recalling the difference the 16-valve engine made Marshall commented: "It was worth about a second a lap. It sounded different, but now we had a problem with reliability of other components. The gearboxes just wouldn't take the power and we had to soften the clutch. We went back to our old Ventora clutch rather than the triple-plate we had been using. You just couldn't change gear smoothly enough for the four-speed box to survive, so we went back to the ordinary Ventora one that we had used for years. This allowed a certain amount of give, and I also had to make sure I treated the box very gently.

"We were having to nurse the car the whole time. When we got oil surge we developed the dry sump system and so on, developing the car the whole time. In fact I was not able to drive it really hard until the time we first used the five-speed box (October 6) for the first attempt at a Super Saloon special event at Silverstone, on the Grand Prix circuit. It was a very wet day and David Howes (driving a 6.9-litre AMC Javelin) won on Firestone wets; I was second".

The DTV mechanics were extraordinarily hardworked by that 16-valve development of the Firenza. It did win on that debut outing at Mallory Park (Dave Millington adding to Vauxhall joy by finishing second), but only after a fraught week. During testing at Snetterton they had trouble with the new engine and the same fault, the bottom end bearings being starved of lubricant, developed in Saturday practice for the Sunday race at Mallory. Gerry Johnstone, Dick Waldock and Geoff Hall hauled the car back to Shepreth from Leicestershire and set to work from 7pm to 4am in order to fire it up. Even then it knocked because of a faulty gudgeon pin. How they found the patience to take it partially apart again and rectify that fault is a mystery, but they did and the car made it back to Leicestershire for the fog-delayed race! Gerry drove the car sympathetically, but even then it was obvious that this was the answer to the increasing speed of rival Escorts. From that 16-valve debut in March to the end of the season it did twenty-seven races, won twenty-one of them and was second (to much bigger capacity cars) in three more.

After the success of the 1972 Group 1 season the organisers originally specified road tyres for the 1973 season, a decision subsequently ameliorated by the appearance of semi-race Klebers and Michelins. However Gerry: " ... refused to drive on road tyres. I thought it was far too dangerous, and I still do. The tyre manufacturers agreed with me: they say for racing you use race tyres and for the road use road tyres. I think its unnecessarily dangerous, so I put my foot down and told Vauxhall that I wouldn't run with road tyres in Group 1 that year.

"I did the one race on January 28 at Brands Hatch with my 1972 car, when they did allow racing tyres, and that was very good. I won the race outright, but that was the last time I raced that car, which was the original DTV Group 1 car. Sadly that car survived - in 2-litre and 2.3-litre racing forms - through all the mayhem of 1972. Sadly because it was then converted to a rally car by Chris Coburn so that I could get some experience for the Tour of Britain. The first rally I did, the Gearbox Rally, I rolled it into a ball and wrote it off. It had survived, while all around had wheels fall off or exploded into flames, then I wrote it off on a rally!" Gerry ended up in the Chester Royal Infirmary with three broken ribs. Vauxhall then decided with DTV that the Tour of Britain was not really a suitable event for G.Marshall as it was of a rallying character: ironically James Hunt/Robert Fearnall won this racing-biased first edition of the Tour in a thundering great 5.7-litre Chevrolet Camaro V8! A thoroughbred racing combination.

That decision obviously played a big part in Marshall's appearance with the Ford team in the 1974 Tour of Britain. Meanwhile another significant influence in 1974 made a humble first contact with racing tarmac ... *Big Bertha*. That was the appropriate name given to a sleek silver Ventora V8 created in the very unusual (and highly impractical as it subsequently materialised) dual role of show and racing car. Vauxhall were preparing to launch a Ventora V8 road car (which failed to materialise) and the special machine created for Gerry consisted of a body cocktail composed in parts of the Ventora steel bodyshell, space frame tubular construction and some outstanding glassfibre work covering the 5-litre Holden V8, alleged to give 495bhp at the time.

The humble first encounter with tarmac arose because publicity pictures were needed of the October-announced project in action for the Motor Show stand and the *Autosport* centrefold colour. As Gerry reports, the debut was a breathless affair: "We hadn't got any driveshafts in the car. We went to Silverstone and Robin Rew took the pictures of me - sitting there with my helmet on - and the car was propelled by six or seven other worthies into Woodcote. It rolled gracefully into camera range with the blokes collapsing, totally breathless and out of the picture. It came out very well on a slow exposure!" The Vauxhall V8 did appear at the Hilton for a press announcement, and on the Vauxhall stand at Earls Court, but " ... didn't turn a wheel in anger in '73", says Gerry.

At the close of the season Gerry had scored the fourth-highest number of wins in British Club Racing, his twenty-three outright victories complemented by a class win taken in Brian 'Slim' Atthews' Capital Motors Viva 1800, and a class title in the Forward Trust series. In fact Marshall's twenty-three overall victories were more than anyone else scored that year, but he was demoted in the *Autosport* chart by Tony Lanfranchi, Bernard Unett and Ivan Dutton, all of them with more *class* wins than Marshall.

Part III: The V8 Vauxhalls

In fact 1974 was not as successful a year as it might have been, the big Ventora taking a long time to sort out before its debut at Silverstone on March 31. Gerry finished the year with seventeen outright wins recorded in the Ventora and the 16-valve Firenza (which took its 50th win in late June) but only three of those victories were in the new V8. Following the fuel crisis of the 1973/74 winter, plans for Vauxhall to market the roadgoing Ventora (with a choice of 4.2 or 4.7-litre Holden V8s) had been abandoned, so some of the impetus behind the project sagged, though DTV themselves fought fiercely to try to overcome some of the problems recounted by Gerry. "I suggested Frank Costin on the design side and he (as an eminent aerodynamicist) was made responsible for the chassis while John Taylor at Vauxhall did the body and its aerodynamics. We stretched the car 10 inches in width and it was all beautifully made. That was the trouble, it was a show car really. I mean it had four opening doors, the door shuts had an absolutely perfect gap, the windscreen fitted and so on. The problem was it was a bit like the driver: overweight and oversize! There was another similarity between us - when extended it got very hot and sweaty as well!

"It was not hard to control, but it was very heavy: the steering and brakes particularly. In retrospect we made a couple of *slight* errors: there was this constant battle between Taylor and Costin. Frank used to reckon he wanted the car up higher to suit the suspension and John wanted it two inches off the ground for the aerodynamics! The best thing that ever happened to that car really was it getting written off, because that enabled us to build *Baby Bertha*." This view was echoed by senior DTV and Vauxhall executives when I spoke to them some years later. Writing in *Motor* in 1974 Marshall's fresh impressions after the debut win from pole position (and a new Silverstone club circuit lap record of 58.2 seconds/99.46mph) were: "The car seemed a bit over-cammed, i.e. the power was coming in too far up the rev-range. As the engine was set up by our antipodean friends perhaps Bill should have installed it upside down? Never mind. The steering is at present far too heavy but we have the answer to this one as well. If you can imagine getting a London bus sideways at 130mph through Woodcote, that's what it was all about the last time we were up there. But unlike a London bus the road-holding once into the corner is very, very good. Bertha isn't deflected by bumps, she's very smooth and exceptionally good on directional stability. This is a tribute to the suspension and the aerodynamics, unlike the Firenza in the early days, which was very twitchy in a straight line". Subsequent memories in 1978 were that the aerodynamics were very good indeed, and that the car was very quick towards the end of each straight. However there were some " ... nasty failures in private practice - things like the De Dion tubes snapping, all fatigued by the weight, which was nearly 27cwt and a *disaster*", in Gerry's view.

One such failure was at Snetterton where, in the opening BRSCC Superloon round on April 14, the front suspension collapsed. "I lost the steering coming out of Riches and just went straight into the Armco". That incident didn't do much damage but Gerry had a narrower escape later in the day " ... when I got involved in another horrendous accident. I was driving Jock Robertson's Magnum, which I sponsored and was driving because it was an international and Jock had not yet gained his international licence. Barrie Williams and I were charging into Russell at the end of the first lap when Zakia Redjep lost it in his Capri: Barry hit him, went up in the air and landed on top of me!" That resulted in a seven car pile up, but only Barrie Williams was badly injured, breaking his ankle. Williams still thinks he suffered the fracture when Gerry hauled him so swiftly from the wreckage!

A rather more amusing Ventora failing came to light at Thruxton: "I let the clutch in, accelerated away in first gear, and the seat slid further and further back! Believe you me, that was no car to drive from the back seat! With the steering and brakes as heavy as they were, pushing on the brakes just gave no retardation at all. I came in and had it fixed, but it immediately happened again and I had to retire. Now I always insist on a rigid seat runner mounting".

It makes my arms ache now to think of applying that much opposite lock in that car! Big Bertha on her only outing at Thruxton, when the seat mounting broke on this aptly nicknamed 5-litre Ventora V8. *Courtesy Colin Taylor.*

The Ventora finally reached the close of its brief public career on August 4. Again it was racing at Silverstone, but this time there was Frank Gardner's mighty Chevrolet Camaro to contend with. Their scrap for the lead on a wet day was doomed: the Ventora had been equipped with new calipers and the usual locking wire had not been applied to retain the pads, some of which abandoned ship at Becketts Hairpin. Gerry was intent on pursuing Gardner at the time and it wasn't until Woodcote, at the end of the long Club straight, that Mr. Marshall made an interesting discovery: *Bertha* really did need all her brakes. The result was a Ventora sufficiently bent to serve as a convincing excuse for cancelling the project. Construction of *Baby Bertha*, based on a Firenza bodyshell began in January 1975, so Gerry reverted to the 16-valve Firenza for the rest of his club racing appearances until May 5 1975, the last time he drove the faithful coupe.

It had been a varied 1974. In March he started a column for *Motor*, in August he was at Kirkistown in Ireland winning an event in Jackie Peterson's 16-valve Firenza, and there was a fortnight's visit to the States, as the guest of General Motors, the legendary styling chief Bill Mitchell having taken a specially strong interest in Gerry's career. This had a due effect on our Vauxhall theme for the chapter because certain parts needed for the Super Saloon programme became a lot easier to procure after Gerry's visit. It was also the year that Gerry demonstrated that he had rather more rough road ability than anyone had imagined. However, he performed his first real demonstration of that talent in a Ford, thus ensuring a place in the Vauxhall Tour of Britain efforts thereafter! He did race a Group 1 Magnum in the RAC Championship, which allowed racing tyres, but the car " ... was totally uncompetitive against the Dolomite that year - though it did go well in the wet at Snetterton towards the end of the year", in Marshall's words.

Gerry's performance on the Tour of Britain in 1974 convinced the powers behind the Vauxhall competition appearances that Marshall was serious about rallying. It was therefore decided to enter him on the Manx International that year. This event uses the narrow, but often fast roads on the Island, including the hillclimb that Marshall used to contest in the TVR, but run-off downhill! Marshall remembers the event well: "Working on the principle that every rally I do, I do with a new navigator, this time we had a young man by the name of Davenport. As everyone knows, he is the King of the Isle of Man, doing all the pace notes that you need.

"You couldn't really have a better man with you for that event. At the time he was the co-driver in the winning car on every alternate year: I can't remember now whether it was his year for a crash or a big win! We drove one of the DTV Magnums, still being prepared by Coburn at the time, and the most notable thing about the car was its complete lack of brakes. In fact, after four stages or so I arrived at a service halt and said there were *no* brakes. They all thought the nasty thoughts they think about racing drivers, but when they jacked it up they found that the disc had actually broken in two!

"We had a tremendous event, part of the winning team prize effort and second in the Group 1 class (to colleague Will Sparrow) and finished 19th overall. I got on very well with John in the car, but the most terrifying thing in the event was coming back from the *Lively Lobster*, an eating establishment on one side of the island. John insisted on driving. He is, without doubt, the world's most terrifying driver!"

Davenport, from his managerial office at Abingdon, also remembered this Manx vividly: "Gerry had the bum car of the two - Will Sparrow had already rejected that one! The brakes let us down all the time, but occasionally they would grab in the right direction, and it would look as if our man had a very smooth line in handbrake turns.

"I thought Marshall was a very professional driver. He didn't get flustered by hearing that Sparrow was going faster, he just pressed on at the right pace for himself. Of course he has superb car control. But there's also a brain in there. He drives exactly on the borderline of his abilities. His performances on the Tour of Britain were another example of his talent - I was most impressed by his conduct in a newish branch of the sport to him", Davenport reported.

Over the years since Gerry and the barman at Brands Hatch had noted the name Nick Whiting in those rallycross results, that same name had crept back into prominence. By 1974 Nick's always immaculate yellow Escort FVC had grown to 1.9-litres and he had scored thirteen outright wins that season, finishing well inside the top twenty clubmen at the close of that year. In 1975 Whiting's 2-litre Escort was up to twenty-four wins in the season. Gerry felt: "Really, Nick and his Ford have been the ones to beat: it has always been a situation where the greatest rivalry existed". In 1975 Gerry rose to third in the *Autosport* club race winners league with twenty-three outright wins, seven class victories allowing him a total tally of thirty to beat his then employee Jock Robertson (Mazda RX3) into fifth position and Whiting to sixth.

Of those twenty-three wins, the brand new car, *Baby Bertha*, provided eighteen. "It was good straight out of the box", Gerry remembers, adding: "We hardly touched a thing on that car from the first test session to its last race - when it was still good enough to thrash Nick Whiting at Thruxton. There's hardly anything you could say about that car, except it was *right*, so right".

Built from the essential running gear of the racing Ventora V8 - front-mounted Holden V8, four-speed Borg-Warner gearbox and De Dion rear end - the Firenza V8 used more standard parts than its forerunner, yet was the wildest-looking and most effective machine to come from DTV. In Gerry's hands it was, " ... unbeatable. It only ever retired once - and that was from its first outing - and I say it was really only ever beaten once: and then we'd just changed over to new rubber. The record books show it beaten again in 1976, but the car that did it (the Chipmunk Imp special driven by Jonathan Buncombe at Silverstone) was later ruled ineligible to race against us! In any case *Baby Bertha*

Marshall, Maidens (a former DTV Chairman) and the literate Leonard Setright. Marshall is saying: "It may not frighten you Leonard but it certainly frightens me". *Courtesy Jeffrey J. Smorley.*

second times, well under the 1 minute 11 seconds record then in force for the fast and windy Norfolk track. Days later it made its debut at the most ironical venue, a FordSport Day at Brands Hatch. The interest it aroused was fantastic and Blydenstein had to work full time answering questions while Gerry Johnstone and the boys got on with sorting out a fuel surge problem that occurred in practice on the twisty Kentish circuit. The car gleamed in the traditional DTV silver, contrasted vividly by Castrol's green and red livery, dominating the Paddock just as Mr. Marshall did. Its striking angular lines and pristine finish belied the fact that Gerry Johnstone, Dick Waldock and Geoff Hall had really drawn it up in the grand old manner, chalk lines on the floor. A Vauxhall engineer affectionately referred to their methods as: "The best DTV eyeballing and thumbwork!"

In that Brands debut it broke a driveshaft when lying third, the failure probably caused by that earlier irregular fuel supply and 200 miles of pre-event testing: under racing conditions *Baby Bertha* rarely went beyond 60 miles, often considerably less. The first win came on June 2 at Mondello Park, but the biggest, and most influential result for DTV's future racing attitude came at the supporting race to the British Grand Prix in July.

It was the Firenza's sixth outing, but it was plain to see that the car and driver were just invincible in the Tricentrol Super Saloon Car Championship, which they duly won that year. None of the opposition - and it included an 8.1-litre Can-Am Chevrolet-engined Corvair - could match Marshall's gusto in finally finding the car of his dreams. It was an ideal partnership, for the mechanics understood Gerry so well that they had provided a car that was well-balanced, even with a front-mounted 5-litre engine. Gerry delighted in thundering round in a car that was spectacular, even if it was only being loaded up to go home!

Gerry's view on the GP-supporting race was: "I was there to drive, no sideways stuff, was suffering from fuel starvation, as was pretty obvious to the spectators."

Baby Bertha was first tested at Snetterton on May 22 and proved capable of 1 minute 8

I did over 60 races in this Hamilton Motors Group 1 Magnum and scored 28 class victories, including one outright win in a Marshall Wingfield sponsored race on the Silverstone Grand Prix circuit.

no mucking about, just get on and win; it was the most important race of the year, after all".

In a damp practice he comfortably netted pole position, but at the start, "Ian Richardson shot off the line in the Corvair and he was ahead as we came up to Copse. He braked early and I was through. From that point on I led all the way". He won by 38 seconds over Alec Poole's screaming 2-litre Skoda special and set a record lap at 110.10mph (1 minute 35 seconds). The race didn't please everyone, *Autosport's* heading summing up the resentment felt by many about the predictable results of the series, calling the race: "Marshall's Monster Bore". The truth was that the opposition comprised mainly: " ... cars that were either badly prepared, poorly developed or incompetently driven", as Marshall was to confirm in a 1977 interview.

The superiority enjoyed by Baby Bertha and Marshall had reached such a pitch by November 1975 that he was able to come into the pits for a half lap breather during a Thruxton televised saloon car race, " ... kick the tyres, look puzzled and rejoin ... we still won and it nearly gave good old Murray Walker a heart attack", Marshall recalls with obvious pleasure. Frequently during 1975 and 1976 Marshall and his mount would toy around looking for someone to play with for a few laps before tooling off into the distance.

G. Marshall was not one to enjoy such a lack of opposition though, and he found the contrast to Super Saloons by becoming involved in Group 1 again in 1975. This time it was Production Saloon Car Racing that he chose, contesting rounds of both the Radio 1 and Britax Championships. This Magnum was sponsored by LBC radio and Hamilton Motors, Vauxhall dealers in Edgware Road, and was launched at a particularly lively party in the showrooms. The success of the party, and of the lady brought in to titillate the jaded press, was almost matched by the car. In its first season (1975) it was usually either first or second in the class and quite often in the top three overall. Gerry did a lot of races in that smart blue and white striped Vauxhall, though it was even more successful in 1976 winning the Radio 1 Championship in its class and taking a superb outright victory in a wet race held on the Silverstone GP circuit. This was an outstanding performance, leaving the bigger capacity BMWs and Opels to follow in the (literal) wake of the Vauxhall.

The Tricentrol Championship was secured for Gerry by September 1975, when he set another new record lap on his way to the title at Oulton Park. By the end of 1976 *Baby Bertha* held lap records at eight circuits, while in 1975 Gerry and *Bertha* had even established a win and fourth place in two *Formule Libre* races. These races were held on the same day as he was contesting saloon car events during a succession of December Brands Hatch club race meetings. This was a pretty remarkable sight as, despite her diminutive nickname, *Baby Bertha* towered over the frail-looking single-seaters of varied ancestry and performance that normally contest such events. By this stage the sight of the Vauxhall hauling into view in a competitor's mirrors was often enough to convince people to move out of the way, especially if they were sitting two feet closer to the ground!

Unhappier outings of 1975 included revisiting the Isle of Man for the Manx Rally, but this time in a non-competing camera car: "We rolled it on the second stage. I always say it was one of the best accidents I've ever had, but there was more publicity at the time than DTV got all year! At least I've finished every rally I've tried since then". In fact a few people may remember that he won a class in a road event; third overall on the Red Dragon Rally in 1976, paired with John Horton of Dunlop, in a Chevette 1200!

The 1975 Tour of Britain was a Vauxhall event for Marshall in an unlucky SMT/Chunky Chickens Magnum 2300. Gerry spent the event " ... trying to destroy the mule so we could get down to the pub!" The misfiring yellow Vauxhall, with Mike Broad as co-driver, provided some spectacular pictures - particularly when suffering frequent punctures, including one on the first 'stage' at Silverstone, but still finished well up in the class, having Barrie Williams' Mazda (" ... *the* worst car I've ever seen", says Marshall) to contend with by the end of an arduous event.

As a whole the 1976 season was his most successful, especially in terms of racing championships. He gave Vauxhall three titles to promote: Overall Tricentrol Super Saloon Car Champion (5.0-litre Firenza V8); first in class for both the Keith Prowse/RAC Saloon Car and BBC Radio 1 Championships. The latter was in the Hamilton Motors car we have already mentioned, but the Prowse/RAC win was taken in a Group 1 Magnum with homologated extras like a five-speed gearbox, six-inch wide alloy wheels and a double Dellorto carburated version of the 2300 engine giving over 180bhp.

Entered by DTV and Castrol, so it was in basically the same silver and contrasting Castrol livery as *Baby Bertha*, the Magnum and Gerry just stuck to the task of trying to beat Andy Rouse's rival for class honours - the Broadspeed Dolomite Sprint. Gerry started off the year with a class win in Tim Stock's rebuilt 1975 Magnum and his progressively improving results led to a new, but similar specification, car being supplied by DTV for the second round of the British Championship. That time he had to give best to Rouse, but in August the two met in battle royal at Mallory Park. In a superb day's racing, watched by a crowd relaxing in the sun, the Marshall versus Rouse duel stood out. It was fabulous entertainment, Gerry having the Dolomite at every corner, crawling alongside under braking for the fast S-curves at the Leicestershire circuit and finally getting by with the aid of his recently acquired rallying expertise: i.e. he used the grass!

Such battles enlivened the rest of the rounds in that championship, culminating in a win over Rouse and a new lap record in the final Motor Show 200 round on Brands Hatch's Grand Prix circuit. He took pole position in a dampish practice, and carried a camera in the Magnum. It was a season during which Gerry had come to respect the driving ability of Colin Vandervell in the Triplex sponsored Capri and the two of them were not only to spend many happy minutes racing against each other, but were also to share a car (Tourist Trophy and Spa 600 Kms 1977). Vandervell actually won that 1976 Motor Show 200 with Marshall an astonishing 1.6 seconds behind, taking second overall

Roger Bannister and Chris Chataway? Definitely not! I show McMahon the way in a charity run for the Roger Williamson Fund, while 'Silverstone Sid' tries to keep up in the Jaguar XJ12 behind!
Courtesy J. St. J. Bloxham.

Here I am attempting to murder the Chunky Chickens/SMT Magnum on the 1975 Tour of Britain. It survived and proved that Chickens have more than nine lives! *Courtesy Colin Taylor.*

for Vauxhall, "... helped by 'Baulkinshaw' (Tom Walkinshaw) and Spice playing with each other and falling off, plus the inevitable explosion in 'Doris' Craft's Capri'', said Gerry.

The biggest disappointment of the year came at Spa-Francorchamps in July, when he drove with Tony Lanfranchi and their blue and orange Magnum had clutch failure after twenty-two and a half of the scheduled twenty-four hours in this Belgian classic. "We were so near", he remembers, "but, as they are meant to say in the movies, that's motor racing!"

However a reward for contesting numerous editions of the Spa-Francorchamps race was to come in 1977, together with a man he first raced with in October 1976 Tourist Trophy. This TT was the race in which the ill-starred Jaguar XJ5.3 coupe made its public bow, but Gerry was busy getting to grips with his troublesome Magnum and appreciating the ability of Australian Peter Brock, who was over on a kind of GM (the firm or the man? It was never explained ...) reciprocal deal. They did not feature in the results on that occasion but the following year's visit to Spa was to prove a lot more profitable, and provide Vauxhall's best-ever international result in ten years of saloon car racing.

Back in 1976, July also provided a much better outing for Vauxhall in the Tour of Britain, Will Sparrow finishing third and Gerry fourth, the first racing driver home in what was to be the last Tour, an event angled toward special stage rallying. Gerry drove a 2.3 Magnum in DTV colours with *Motoring News'* then-current journalist/co-driver Michael Greasley, a pairing that was often to be seen grinning madly out of a Vauxhall surrounded by the airborne debris from another haybale. Whether Greasley was too busy giggling to direct his driver, or whether Marshall was too busy laughing at 'Grizzly's' sophisticated wind orchestration is unknown. In between the jollity they got down to some pretty serious stage motoring, Gerry setting fastest time on the last stage and being the only racing driver in the top five placings: significantly Ford used only rallying drivers

Tweaked up together: Old Nail and I at one of our last DTV appearances. I now have the car as a memento of those memorable years and 63 wins. *Courtesy Colin Taylor.*

for their RS2000s that year, and it was one of their two Finnish aces (Ari Vatanen) who won this event. Marshall suggests that: "We should have won. The Magnums were really well prepared and very quick. Of course most people only remember all the aggravation we had with James Hunt, the law and inconveniently-located trees in Norfolk. If it had not been for those gearbox changes (remember I had two in the event), I really think we could have won. A great pity, for the Tour was one of the events I enjoyed doing and I was very sorry to see it end".

Apart from the regular number of 'Man of the Meeting' awards won by Marshall, 1976 was a particularly good year to gauge his popularity with the public, or those that read *Autosport*. That magazine organised a poll amongst its readers, asking them to vote for the sixteen drivers they would most like to see in an Escort Celebrity race backing up the Brands Hatch Grand Prix in July.

How Marshall had become the spectators' favourite can be judged from the voting order, for he won with 906 to 765 for the attractive Divina Galica, Rupert Keegan gaining 654 votes in third place. It was interesting that so many racing fans especially wanted to see Roger Clark out again on the circuit, but unfortunately he was too committed to rallying to appear. Perhaps Roger was lucky, for in the event: "It was a diabolical race, just untalented rock-apes barging into each other for the pleasure of smashing the cars up. Lanfranchi and I both retired, there was just no point in trying to race", says Gerry.

Away from competition, significant things had been happening at Shepreth. In 1975 Bill Blydenstein was asked to take overall responsibility for DTV, and that included all the rallying activities being undertaken by Chris Coburn's concern at Banbury. Inevitably this changed in 1976 and Blydenstein agreed to take on the Vauxhall rallying programme, beginning with the Magnums from Coburn, but rapidly progressing to the point where they had suggested and implemented the construction of the rallying Chevette, complete with 240-horsepower, 16-valve engine. The Chevette appeared on the RAC Rally in November and was to have much significance on Gerry's racing in 1977. "I had nine wins in *Baby Bertha* that year, won the Tricentrol title and the two other class titles, but I knew the rallying had to change things. When they paid a fortune for Pentti Arikkala to drive the Chevette in 1977, it had to come from somewhere. So you could say I had forebodings about my tenth season racing Vauxhalls, or you could say things looked blanking grim ...!"

In fact the season was not all bad, although he did far less races for Blydenstein than at any time since the first faltering steps ten years previously. Baby Bertha was aired only twice in Britain, and once in Denmark where it had to face up to a field of Porsches, including turbocharged 935s, around, " ... that tiny Mickey Mouse circuit at Jyllandsring. I found that hard work: I could get alongside the Porsches under braking, or actually in the corners, but traction out was a problem. Anyway, we finished fourth or thereabouts which wasn't bad in a car that filled the circuit on its own, never mind the bloody Porsches!

"We also took the Group 1 Magnum along to Jyllandsring to race against Erik Hoyer, who's won the Championship for the past seven years, they tell me! He has a really well-sorted Escort RS2000 running on just the right tyres for the funny surface they have there. I thought the Magnum's torque would see us alright however tight the track was, but I was wrong. We did a series of five lap sprints which were pretty hectic. On one of them I started from the front row alongside Erik and they reprimanded me for my start: I think they are still writing to somebody in Britain about the 300 kroner fine! In another session I led until the last corner, last lap, then blasted Erik nipped through to win. Finally we were put out when the gearbox, an old rally unit, had the main shaft break.

"So far as the RAC Group 1 Championship Magnum was concerned the car was as bad in 1977 as it was good in 1976. There was no interest up at the works on the management side, they'd simply got too much on their plate with the rallying". In fact that 1976 RAC Magnum startled everyone at an early season Silverstone Championship round of 1977, leading Capri chargers like Gordon Spice, Chris Craft and Colin Vandervell from the start. It held onto its cheeky advantage until the Hangar straight asserted that 220bhp and 3-litres had uses compared to 2.3-litres and under 190-horsepower. Gerry subsequently had a puncture and really got angry and determined about the situation. His class was dominated, as it was to be for the rest of the year, by Tony Dron's Dolomite, but Gerry broke the class record *four times* on the way to leaving it at 1 minute 47.11 seconds and 98.55mph. He finished the race in sixth place, having fallen as low as nineteenth at one stage.

In subsequent rounds there were fewer class rewards than before, though, as Gerry succinctly sums up: "It wasn't quite as bad as I expected. We had two tyre failures and we got beaten by Jeff Allam's Magnum twice. There just wasn't the will or the cash to go testing and bring our Magnum up to scratch. With development there's no reason why the Magnum could not have carried on giving the Dolomites, and the rest, trouble but it simply wasn't on. I should have won at Donington, the first time the RAC blokes went up for a Championship round. I was leading when a halfshaft broke".

His other Magnum, the faithful Hamilton Motors machine scored regular class wins in the Britax Production Saloon Car Championship.

Ironically the highlight of the Vauxhall's career came in its last DTV season. Held over July 23 and 24 from three o'clock on Saturday afternoon to finish twenty-four hours later on Sunday, 1977's Spa-Francorchamps test of saloon car endurance held its usual quota of dramatics. Quite simply the event is *the* prestige one for saloon cars in Europe, regularly attracting between eighty and one hundred thousand spectators. Traditionally the preserve of BMW, though Ford of Germany did well when they were represented, the 1977 race looked as though it would provide a British victory at one stage. However that car, Gordon Spice's Capri, crashed and it was left to Vince Woodman/Jonathan Buncombe and Gerry Marshall/Peter Brock to chase the winning BMW of Eddy Joosen/Jean Claude Andruet. At the halfway stage Marshall/Brock were not even in the top ten, having been delayed for thirteen minutes by a faulty starter motor connection.

As described earlier they survived a gloomy and typically Ardennes early morning deluge by switching to Dunlop and Michelin tyres, putting them back on an even footing with their Alfa Romeo rivals. For the closing stages of the race I can do no better than quote the report of *Motoring News* reporter David Smith. "Behind, Marshall had taken over from the impressive Brock, and quickly stifled the threat from the Alfetta. But Big Gerry was not content with a mere class win. Lap after lap he threw the Magnum round the circuit with tremendous verve, visibly gaining all the time on Woodman's second place Capri.

"The crowd were loving every minute of it, and rose as one with thirty minutes to go as the silver Vauxhall rushed past the pits, several lengths in front of its Ford rival, Marshall's hand held aloft in celebration".

Marshall's verdict was: "The truth is that there is a shortage of people who can drive saloons to an international standard over a twenty-four hour race. I know we would not have had our finishing place at Spa if it had not been for the fact that other drivers tired faster than we did. Both Peter and I were as quick at the finish as we were at the start. You can be so easy on a car that any well-prepared saloon should finish the twenty-four hour event now. You've got time to think and sort things out".

Those were the words of a Spa ace, though. For most drivers the track presents a daunting challenge, one that has been refused by Grand Prix drivers since 1970. In finishing second (winning the class of course) Marshall and Brock averaged 100.52mph for the 2412.5miles they covered in that day and night of consistent speed. They also led the Belgian DTV team to the coveted *Coupe du Roi* team award. Remember that is over what we would class as an A-road with one chicane and a hairpin. This gives an idea of the high speeds involved elsewhere on the track: it's rather like batting across East Anglia with hills and 130mph corners!

The October 27 1977 issue of *Autosport* carried the apparently inevitable obituary to the DTV-Marshall racing programme. The statement from Bill Blydenstein at Shepreth simply said: "Dealer Team Vauxhall plans for 1978 do not include a circuit racing programme. We intend to concentrate on engineering development and take a close look at all forms of motoring competition. We are happy to announce that Gerry Marshall will remain with DTV in a consulting capacity. His wide experience and expertise will continue to be of great value to us".

Gerry himself had only heard the news a few days before the telex was sent out and it was obviously a heavy blow. "I couldn't feel bitter toward Bill, we've done too much together, though I was upset that the rallying obsession should throw out what had been - and still could be - a very successful racing programme. Rallying's a good sport, and nobody enjoys it more than me (in fact I even hoped I might be able to take it up with DTV ... why not, worse things have happened at sea?) but to boot out all that racing experience, that seemed all wrong to me".

Naturally there was some correspondence in the press over his departure, one letter simply ending: "There will never be anybody who drives Vauxhalls better", and summing up the appeal the combination had in over ten years' racing. A more cynical clipping came from *Autosport* and currently adorns the walls of the Marshall-Wingfield offices: " 'I want you to tell that guy Gerry Marshall that he's Mr. Goddam Vauxhall - we love him' Mr. Hal Carpenter of Vauxhall's Marketing Division, two days before DTV's racing operations closed down". There is no doubt in my mind that Vauxhall were not being cynical in that case, it's just that General Motors' public awareness is often slow in reacting, a kind of handicap inherited from their gigantic parent corporation in America.

The last race for *Baby Bertha* came on October 30th, appropriately at one of Gerry's

What it was all about. Nick Whiting and I sort each other out at Brands. *Courtesy J. St. J. Bloxham and Colin Taylor.*

There's no truth in the rumour that they had to make Bertha this wide to get all the signwriting on! Baby Bertha is the centre of attention on her debut at the FordSport day, May 1975.

She never was that smart again ... Baby B wheels out of the Brands Hatch infield into battle for the first time.

favourite British circuits, the fast Thruxton course set almost on Salisbury Plain and the headquarters of the British Automobile Racing Club. It was an eight lap, nineteen odd miles, event for 'special Saloons', the odd 'Superloon' title having faded into obsolescence along with the championship at the end of 1976. Equally appropriate was that it was Nick Whiting, now in his fierce Escort Mk2 with a 3.4-litre Ford V6 motor, who sat alongside Gerry on the front row, Nick having practised just 0.1 second faster. In the race the yellow Escort could only head Marshall once and it suffered a slow puncture toward the end, " ... so Marshall reigned supreme and was given a royal reception ...", in the *Motoring News* account while Gerry added: "It proved how competitive we were, right to the bitter end. Nick was still nowhere near our times". In fact Whiting's fastest lap was in 1 minute 21.3 seconds (104.32mph) as compared to Gerry's Firenza V8 record of 1 minute 20.4 seconds (105.49mph), set in October 1976. Because it had scarcely appeared in 1977, *Baby Bertha's* lap record total fell sharply, though it still held four at the end of 1977.

In a very interesting aside the following year, Marshall confirmed that the legendary *Baby Bertha* was sold, " ... for £8500 to Paul Heywood-Halfpenny. A real bargain as he also got the spares, including the second engine and gearbox. In fact the car had been sold just prior to the Thruxton finale. The car's ruined now, painted black and the telltale has seen rpm peaks that beat even Jeremy Lawrence's testing record with the Ventora!"

Gerry did not sit and mope over the departure of DTV and his V8 lady friend, hopping over to appear for the last time in his Hamilton Motors Magnum in the next race at Thruxton that day. He fought a typical, hard scrap with John Lyon's Alfetta for fourth place, finally suffering a puncture and the consolation of a faster lap than the Alfa Romeo driver. He was also awarded the Phil Winter Memorial Trophy by the marshals at that meeting, one of the many awards he won from a body of volunteers who rate him just as highly as the paying spectator.

As he drove home from that Thruxton farewell, Gerry must have been contemplating what might have been in the next decade. It was not to be, but for your edification dear reader, in the next Chapter we expose: "The Car That Never Raced", together with those Vauxhalls that did ...

The car that
never was

"If DTV had been an operation without Gerry Marshall, both the results and the chance to introduce exciting Vauxhall road cars would have been lost. From design to production they know his name: we would never have been able to try an exercise like the 'droop snoot' Firenza without Gerry's success. And, without the 'droop snoot', we would never have got to the stage of making the Chevette HS2300''. These words came from some of the engineering occupants of the Vauxhall engineering and styling centre at Luton. Encased securely within that high-security establishment, a glittering multi-storey office block, all one can see are engineers surrounded by their clicking calculators. Most of them are grappling with the tortuous problems set by current vehicle safety and exhaust emissions requirements for the vehicles the public will want in the 1980s, and beyond. However, within every big organisation the Enthusiasts lurk.

At Vauxhall the Enthusiast is in a more difficult position than a counterpart outside General Motors. Since competition became a dirty word back in the States there have been GM employees all over the World who have massaged, bent, levered and generally bucked the system. Quite often the Enthusiasts, by their very thrusting nature, became very successful company men too. In the story of the car that never was, Vauxhall styling director Wayne Cherry was just such a man. His passion was primarily directed at Formula 1, but underneath him was a blunt-speaking Australian called John Taylor; he demonstrated an uncanny knack over the years for actually getting down and creating the often sensational lines of the racing Vauxhall saloons. He started off by producing the wheelarch extensions on Vivas and is then generally acknowledged to be the man responsible for the racing Firenza, its subsequent 'droop snoot' line blending in with the curvaceous sidelines. The Ventora ("As he was a styling man they put him on the aerodynamics: as Costin was an aerodynamicist, they put him on the chassis!" Gerry commented earlier); the Firenza V8 and the stillborn Cavalier V8, all were creations of this unlikely representative of the Enthusiasts.

"*Baby Bertha* had come to the end of her usefulness and we knew 1976 would have to be her last season", according to one Vauxhall executive, who added: "The Firenza was no longer sold and the same argument applied to the Magnum coupé in Group 1. We had to stop using them and we discussed what should succeed Baby Bertha frequently in 1976". DTV liason engineer Roy Cook felt: "We should have a Chevette, a real Luton-built *Vauxhall*. Two things altered my mind, the first was that 1977 decision to concentrate a 101 percent effort on the Chevette in rallying. The second was the decision that Vauxhall would build the Cavalier in Luton, so the discussion between interested parties at Vauxhall and DTV agreed on Cavalier."

Concrete plans for the car were laid down in February 1977, though a couple of options remained over the gearbox location and engine type at the early stages. One all important point was that it had to bear more relationship to the standard product in looks than had *Baby Bertha* - though that car was really unjustly criticised,for it had more standard Firenza coachwork than the previous Ventora, on which hardly a panel was shared with the production car. *Baby Bertha* used a surprising amount of Firenza content, I was told. To keep the proportions right the styling people had to widen the car by a foot, matching the inevitable track increase with huge racing tyres and wheels installed. "The body concept was simple, a glassfibre envelope over a monocoque chassis designed by Jo Marquart: a front-engined Formula car with a body, in other words", in one executive's account.

At this stage they were still juggling with the possibility of using a 2.5-litre turbocharged engine and a rear mounted transaxle transmission and gearbox. That 1974 visit Marshall had paid to the States had left a residue of goodwill toward such projects, especially with Vice President and styling centre boss at that time, William L. Mitchell. Excellent contacts in America provided a source from which to supply examples of the aluminium 8.1-litre Reynolds-Chevrolet V8 engines, famous for their one-time monopoly of the SCCA Can-Am sports racing series, when installed in the back of bright orange McLarens.

"Since the car was planned to weigh a good deal less than the Firenza four-cylinder and those V8 engines could give 700-horsepower, we reckoned it should be pretty quick!" was Gerry's view of the car's potential with the conclusion: "All the cars John has had a hand in for us have been beautiful, but the Cavalier, aahhh, what a cracker it looked. Even though it wasn't finished for photographic work, it still looked so right".

What killed the Cavalier racing programme? Sources at the factory and elsewhere say it was not just the demands of rallying - though the 101 percent effort demanded of the Shepreth personnel obviously drained away the resources of what has been described as "the small tight-knit DTV community". The feeling inside Vauxhall seems to have favoured an international approach to replace the previous emphasis on club racing. It is said that Bill Blydenstein was extremely apprehensive over the Group 1 Magnum's racing programme in Britain and abroad, all against the finest opposition in Europe, and that Bill was both surprised and delighted when Marshall proved so competitive with the Broadspeed Dolomite drivers in 1976. Blydenstein actually rated the 1977 Spa performance as: "Vauxhall's first real international race result". One engineer put it to me: "Introducing the Cavalier to club racing and spending the kind of money needed for that project seemed like overkill to many of us. Funnily enough the press never gave us a hard time over our club racing success - we always were left with the message that Vauxhall's presence was a welcome relief from Ford and Leyland - no, it was really the criticism of the other competitors that made us withdraw from the category".

The thought that they might one day be too successful to continue in club racing can hardly have dominated the minds of Mr. Marshall and Mr. Blydenstein when they first joined forces, ten years before the Cavalier was abandoned. Through regular articles written by Blydenstein, Roger Bell and even myself, we can look back and see what they had in 1967. The December 2 issue of *Motor* was getting to grips with what was to be a series of Blydenstein Vauxhall tests. Then we could see a white and orange-striped Viva standing on Pearce Magna alloy wheels of 4.5 inch rim width. Externally the body looked like today's Group 1 cars (though the use of 12 inch diameter front wheels and 13 inch diameter rears was a bit unusual!) but the underbonnet installation of a single twin-choke Weber IDA had required some of the bonnet cross bracing being cutaway. The interior lacked any trim, saving an estimated hundredweight and bringing the total down close to 16 cwt. That was powered by an estimated 95bhp, produced from the pushrod 1258cc unit. Less than ten years later they had a device weighing 20cwt and propelled by 460 to 476bhp, depending which of the two supplied V8s were used in *Baby Bertha*. Now that's progress! So was the fact that in 1967 Roger Bell found the car had been managing about 100mph on the Silverstone Club straight, whereas almost exactly eight years later he was having to back off at 7000rpm and 147mph on any decent straight! Even then *Baby*

Bertha was not geared for her normal 7500rpm at slightly under 160mph, usually recorded before Stowe on the Silverstone Grand Prix track.

The two cars from the beginning and end of Blydenstein racing history had a four-speed gearbox in common, but where Bill and the team merely had the Muncie-shifting Borg-Warner gearbox " ... procured from some GM friends abroad", Bill personally designed the first close-ratio gearbox for the 1258 Shaw & Kilburn Special HB. This was introduced to the car in 1968 and Bill provided an interesting table for readers of *Hot Car* to see the improvement. It went like this: Standard, first, 3.76:1 - rpm gap on changing at 7000rpm, 2870; second, 2.22 - rpm drop 2570; third, 1.405 - rpm drop to fourth (which was direct 1.0:1 ratio in both cases), 2020rpm. Modified ratios on the same basis offered: First, 2.96:1-2880rpm drop; second, 1.74-1950rpm drop and third to fourth on third gear's 1.225 ratio left a 1420rpm loss. It is also interesting to note the comparison in Snetterton lap times over the years down from just under two minutes when Bill first realised that he could drive the thing faster than the hired driver (not Gerry) to under 1 minute 9 seconds at the same circuit when *Baby Bertha* was first wheeled out. Unfortunately Snetterton was severely altered in several respects during that period, but worth quoting as Snetterton has always been home to the DTV team and its drivers. In terms of then and now Silverstone Club track, consisting of a simple three corner layout showed that the 1258 used to lap in 1 minute 16 seconds while *Baby Bertha* managed 56.2 seconds!Those are DTV times, not official records and are given to show the dramatic progress they made on the technical front.

The introduction of the Viva GT with its 2-litre sohc engine gave Gerry and Bill what they needed as a basis to go out and try to win races outright. Power outputs measured on different test beds are notoriously misleading, though they have their own at Shepreth now. For comparison I will quote the old figures "bandied about" (Gerry's apt description) in the process designed to impress the opposition and the media, but which often had little factual basis as development and racing were such a hectic simultaneous task that proper horsepower tests could rarely be conducted. The 2-litre probably had less than 120bhp when it made its debut, the modifications beginning with a pair of 45DCOE twin-choke sidedraught carburettors feeding the slant engine, which had a certain amount of spit and polish applied to its inlet and exhaust porting and had been fitted with new inlet and exhaust manifolding. After a late 1968 season debut, November saw an estimated extra 20bhp extracted from two successive improvements in camshaft profiles. That improved camshaft allowed the car to rev to 7600rpm in top gear during wet Silverstone test sessions and really made the car feel more of a 'racer'. It certainly looked more the part than the pushrod Viva ever had, wheelspats making their first appearance to cover wider wheels by the 1969 introduction of a new but still Shaw and Kilburn sponsored, machine.

When Tecalemit-Jackson received a complete engine to make up a race-installation fuel injection system late in 1968 it was thought the unit gave " ... about 150bhp". For Boxing Day Brands, right at the end of 1968, Gerry had a quoted: "155bhp at 6500rpm", and he certainly behaved as if there was another 100 on top of that. From the start Marshall headed a Falcon round the club circuit layout, before bowing spectacularly to the inevitable passage of 4.7 litres. Even then he was able to harry the big Ford effectively, so the 2-litre was literally taking the team into the big league.

In 1969 compression went up from 9.1 to 10.3:1 on the original car, but reliability was more of a problem than the claimed 170bhp. Only when Cooper's Mechanical Joints were able to supply some special head sealing gaskets were these higher compression problems anything like solved. The 'lightweight' club car introduced that year had 200 claimed bhp by the close of 1969, closer-ratio gears and glass-fibre panels, including the boot, bonnet " ... and passenger's door in my car", says Marshall. "I like my driver's door in steel with hooligans all about me!"

The closer ratios - first, second and third - were achieved by altering only one set of

It was still a bit damp when we went out in the supporting race to the British GP 1975! This pretty picture shows Bertha resisting the temptation to paddle and getting on with the job of scoring a significant victory.

Barrie Williams (centre) worries about a young lady's goose-pimples. Taken at the magnificent launching party for the Hamilton Motors Magnum, Rex Greenslade (left) and I look on. *Courtesy Motofoto.*

gears, those of the first motion shaft and its layshaft partner. Unfortunately the earliest attempts produced errors in the helix angles and led to trouble in that area to compliment the problems they had already overcome in beefing up the rear axle casing and components. DTV eventually settled for a locked differential, though a proper limited slip differential did appear for the Firenza. The halfshafts were stress relieved and replaced with monotonous regularity. Gerry Johnstone, " ... became very adept at changing head gaskets between practice and the race", according to all observers. That four-speed gearbox and the use of bigger Ventora front discs and calipers lasted well into the era of the Firenza coupé. The suspension of all the four-cylinder Viva GTs and Firenzas was remarkably little altered from basic principles: the Viva did not even use racing Rose joints for most of its racing life, while the Firenza of 1972 still had only the front end Rose-jointed. In both cases the front wishbones were strengthened, the top A-arm being re-drilled to provide negative camber. At the back the usual four link suspension system was used, an anti-roll bar first appearing in 1969. Naturally the rim widths progressed over the years - and Goodyears were adopted with the 2-litre engine. By 1971, the last year of the Viva GT racing appearances, the cars were on 10 inch wide Minilite wheels. That stayed much the same on the Firenza while it had the single overhead camshaft motor, but in 1973 it got not only the 16-valve engine mentioned in the racing chapter, but also rear disc brakes and 12 inch wide Minilites. The aerodynamics were improved gradually on the Firenza, which initially was rather twitchy for Gerry to drive. Finally it appeared with droop nose and rear spoiler, which improved both speed and stability.

The other very significant Viva racing development was in the capacity of the engines. In March 1969 Blydenstein initiated a programme to build a 2.3-litre version of the engine using pre-production Vauxhall 2.3 pistons and a crankshaft reclamation process to weld and grind the crankpins off-centre to provide extra stroke. Blydenstein

All pictures of this occasion - the 1975 DTV party - were suppressed and you see why with this dreadful cast. Left to right, they are: Barrie Williams, Will Sparrow, Alan Maidens, Chris Coburn while I am the one in the smooth headgear. *Courtesy Colin Taylor.*

had previously used this process on his Mini 850 racer, but the problem was that the Viva's crankshaft was of cast iron. Bill laughs about some of the resultant explosions now - "The *biggest* clouds of smoke *ever* seen on the Snetterton straight" - but the extra torque and a hopeful 200bhp made persistence worthwhile. Even in 1969 though the original process showed its potential, Gerry chasing the talented Graham Birrell (1.9 Escort Twin Cam) for four laps at the Mallory Park FordSport day, actually beating that car and driver at Oulton Park a few weekends later. Then the engine was equipped with larger exhaust valves and a new fuel injection cam. During that winning Cheshire performance Gerry also demonstrated the unit's massive torque. "The gearlever came off in my hand at the start", reported Gerry, "and so I could only use third and top on the stubby remains".

The solution to the reliability of the big capacity engine came from 1970 when, in Blydenstein's words: "We were also able to get some early 2.3 crankshafts, which I feel are the strongest of their kind in the business. We never looked back from that point on". The original engines measured 2.2-litres with a production bore, stroked crankshaft and standard pistons. A small boring job for racing pistons brought 2.3-litres (2310cc on the 97mm bore and a 77mm stroke) while a subsequent version included 2.5-litres from the production 92.5mm bore coupled to an 87mm stroke instead of the production 69.24mm: the 2.6 litre stretch was the biggest ever used and that combined the bigger bore and longer stroke. Power outputs quoted by TJ at the time ranged from 179bhp at 7000rpm (2-litre) up to 210bhp for the 2.6-litre, with nearly the same amount of torque being developed as well. It was the latter engine that took Gerry to victory at Mondello Park in 1971 against Hill's then-all-conquering Capri V8 and Brodie's 2.1-litre Escort Twin Cam.

Viva technical development stopped with a bang, or series of bangs, at Lydden Hill, as you have already heard. The technical people were not that sorry to see the high drag Viva body shape go in favour of the Firenza, which was the first machine to get full Vauxhall wind-tunnel testing for the beautiful Styling Centre body. So it literally was as good as it looked with its fashionable massive body extensions, smoothly blended into a coupé that even had tinted glass: truly a TV star's car! Subsequently all the DTV racing V8 saloons were wind-tunnel tested too, though John Taylor created the face of Baby Bertha from, " ... beneath a growing pile of plaster", as one team man remembers it.

Built up gradually during 1971, the Thames Firenza was always a favourite car with the team, Gerry Johnstone particularly remembering it as: "The most attractive car we did". Gerry Marshall voted its extreme reliability as the outstanding quality - "I have to think hard to remember it retiring from more than two races. A great credit to everyone at Shepreth, that car. I always point out that I never put a scratch on Old Nail ... the boys did more damage dropping it off the trailer!'" Incidentally, the Thames TV Firenza marked a new colour scheme for the team, the main body remaining silver, but the contrasting stripe being in blue, right up until the Thames TV 'sponsorship' (mainly publicity to tie in with the launch of the *Drive In* programme) was dropped for the 1972 season. Then the car went to silver with black bonnet plus orange stripe, and subsequently appeared, after Castrol had become sponsors of DTV (including the rally team), in silver and Castrol livery. The Vivas started off white and orange of course, but when DTV was formed in 1971 they briefly appeared in silver and orange too, before the Lydden Hill catastrophe. Historians may care to note that two Vivas were sold, in their wrecked state, to John Pope and Gerry Johnstone. Both were subsequently rebuilt, Johnstone's as a Firenza. *Old Nail*, the remarkable racing Firenza, was presented to Gerry officially right at the end of 1977, to add to his mini collection - and Gerry won a Brands Hatch Sprint BTD with it less than a week into the New Year. Typically he also sold his first Chevette HS2300 at the same sprint, following a class-winning day with the production Vauxhall.

Clive Richardson, then of *Cars & Car Conversions* now Deputy Editor of *MOTOR SPORT* provided a fascinating outsider's account of the Firenza in 1972, when it was estimated that Blydenstein could build a complete replica for £4500, exclusive of purchase tax: the 2.5-litre, 210bhp"tractor engine"represented £1200 of the cost. At that time the emphasis was still on the number of standard or standard-based components in use - then estimated at 80 percent in the case of the racing Vauxhall and under 25 percent in the make up of racing Ford saloons. The fascinating part of the account lies in the ease with which this experienced track tester was able to record 1 minute 44.0 seconds around the old Snetterton layout, as compared with the 1 minute 41.4 seconds which was Gerry's best performance at the time. "A surprisingly easy car to adapt to - and go quickly in, up to a point", was the tester's verdict. Clive also discovered the hard way that the Firenza's high speed oversteer, Mr. Marshall's forte, was the characteristic at which Mr. Marshall earned his pennies and slashed those seconds away from the lap time.

The 2.5-litre sohc motor was used for that test and for a year after the Firenza's first race in September 1971. The successor was another sohc unit, this time of 2.3 litres which was to tie in nicely with the Vauxhall introduction of the 2300 Firenza, which was also homologated into Group 1. Called the Clubman engine in full racing guise, the 2.3 capacity allowed 7500rpm with safety. The 2.5-litre was really meant to stay below 7000 revs and Bill recalled that maximum power was actually at 5800 rpm, though press material usually referred to a more sporty 6500rpm, presumably to convince the others it was a racing motor! Of the 2.3-litre engine Gerry found: "Although down on bhp it was very much up on torque and throttle response, giving the very agile Firenza a decided advantage out of the corners". That capacity utilised a number of Vauxhall-based components, such as the cast-iron crankshaft and lightened and polished connecting rods. A change to a steel crankshaft for the engine only came in 1975, but the dry sump lubrication was introduced after the 16-valve Lotus head (first offered to Bill in 1968 by Chapman's company) was adopted in March 1973. The dry sump allowed the engine to live under such arduous conditions, even with the large numbers of modified production parts that were used. In 1974 the Firenza received two final finishing touches, the five-

John Wingfield.

speed ZF gearbox and 'droop snoot' bodywork.

The Ventora was conceived in May 1973 and had to be ready for press and public presentations by October 1. Like the Cavalier that did not race, the Ventora V8 was a masterpiece of the stylist's art. Although it looked like a road car and had a compromised linkage to the rear De Dion layout in order to avoid intruding upon the centre section that was the heart of the Vauxhall Ventora road car message, it was actually considerably wider than the production car, a large strip being inserted in the centre to pull the body line out and over those 15 inch wide rear wheels and 12 inch wide fronts. The rear layout included a Jaguar rear differential (3.54:1 ratio) and Jaguar driveshafts. The De Dion layout was supported by a square tube subframe, and either of the two 5-litre Repco-Holden V8 engines were similarly cradled at the front. Standard XJ6 brake calipers and non-ventilated inboard discs were used at the rear. The bigger and thicker, ventilated front discs used aluminium four-piston calipers and Ferodo DS11 pad material.

The front suspension was of unequal length wishbones with inclined shock absorbers and springs by Koni. The suspension fabrication had to be substantially modified after the Snetterton failure, though there was bound to be a fundamental stress problem with long lower arms stretching into the deep inset of the German BBS alloy wheels, especially as these arms were carrying 27cwt. Both front and rear had anti-roll bars and there was *107*

A lot of Autosport readers voted for this sight, G. Marshall in a celebrity Escort at the British GP, Brands, 1976, but the race was a disaster. *Courtesy J. St. J. Bloxham.*

Driving Pete Hall's Capri 3-litre to a win and a record lap at Thruxton, 1976. *Courtesy Evan Selwyn-Smith.*

"You did say use all the road Mike!" Mike Greasley and I finished fourth overall on the 1976 Tour of Britain with the DTV Magnum 2300. *Courtesy LAT.*

One way to stop DTV mentioning the cost of tyres ... I am told this picture of myself and the Group 1 Magnum in RAC Championship sums up our appeal to the crowds.

pretty well the full Formula car facility to adjust the car to track conditions in respect of the suspension. At the rear the De Dion layout had two lower leading arms and one top trailing arm for location plus a Panhard rod. The shock absorbers and coil springs were vertically mounted in line with the trailing arms, not as far outboard as they could have been owing to the massive intrusion of the wheelarches needed to contribute to that production car image. The car's sleek good looks - it had a new paint job between its press showing and Earls Court - owed a great debt to Mike Rawlings and Barry Shepherd of Rawlson Plastics who were to prove their worth on the glassfibre front section, tail and provision of the requisite four glassfibre doors, fully trimmed. Just the removal of the rain guttering and the substitution of flush-fitting perspex all round made the car look so much more appetising. Apart from an integral nose/bib blending into the front arches, these were the only obvious aerodynamic aids on this subtle car. Even when the Ventora was being built at Shepreth, Gerry Johnstone was itching to do things his way, so when the Ventora was heavily damaged in that Silverstone accident Johnstone saw his chance: "I could do it my way, I was *certain* we could make a car here that would be an outright winner, and that's what we needed. Gerry M had been too many years without a car to win outright on the faster tracks. Do you know how we got that body shape for *Baby Bertha*? I'll tell you. We took a standard Firenza centre section, laid out all the bits we were going to use from *Big Bertha* - engine, gearbox, De Dion rear end and wheels; we modelled over the basic components with wire mesh and string to get roughly what we wanted ... but John Taylor made it all come right, and he wasn't above rolling up his sleeves and getting stuck in with us. It took eleven weeks to build that car with myself, Dick Waldock and Geoff Hall just getting on with it: precious little theory; just carry on until we had a car. When it was finished we virtually rolled it out of here and up to Snetterton. Gerry took it round *five seconds* under the record, straight out of the box. I remember asking him if he wanted the shock absorber setting changed and he just told me to leave it! I don't think we ever did more than fiddle with the suspension from that day on, it was an amazing car".

The suspension was basically the same as before, but the rear De Dion was located by three leading arms, the top trailing arm being dispensed with, though the replacement leading arm still located above the differential. The Repco-Holden engine, with its cast iron Chevrolet ancestry and Lucas fuel-injection, weighed 655lbs on its own, but was set so far back in the chassis that the weight distribution (and there was seven *hundredweight* less of *Baby Bertha*!) was more akin to a mid-engine car. The Borg-Warner T10S gearbox was mated up to a special BRD competition propshaft, but the Salisbury differential, complete with limited slip operating at 150lbs.ft, remained.

When John Nicholson started maintaining the Repco-built V8s he cured the misfire that had ailed the Ventora's early outings with a modified Rover V8 distributor hitched up to a Lumenition electronic-ignition system. The power output figures also became a lot more realistic than the 500 odd previously spoken of: today the key team members say that the car always had at least 460bhp, this minimum figure comparing with the 476bhp at 7400rpm and 380lbs.ft torque quoted for a freshly built motor. The angular, slab-sided bodywork around the cockpit looked as though it could have been prepared with side-radiators in mind, but the only cooling at the back concerned ducting for the differential and inboard back discs.

A large, sloping front radiator was fitted with a 24-row oil cooler also inclined in front of it. The body consisted of an all-steel centre section, including the Firenza doors, with glassfibre tail and bonnet section over the square tube spaceframe, built onto the back and front bulkheads of the reinforced Luton centre section. Although Frank Costin did not play the major role that he had in the Ventora's construction he did switch the front suspension over to inboard operation and he can also be credited for the largely similar De Dion rear end layout.

The only track test performed before Baby Bertha was sold was by Roger Bell, then at

Even a Broadspeed-tuned Dolomite needs a power boost now and again. I help Andy Rouse out of the Mallory Park hairpin before the Magnum and I went on to score our first win over the factory-backed Dolomite in 1976. *Courtesy J. St. J. Bloxham.*

I am told this is one of 10,000 such pictures! Silverstone Tourist Trophy 1976. *Courtesy Colin Taylor.*

Motor (now freelancing having left Vauxhall) who said, among other things, that the Firenza V8 was : " ... a relatively easy car to drive. It must be Gerry's flamboyant style that makes it look as though the machine is always on the verge of winning its confrontation with man. It's not like that at all".

Gerry simply opined of his faithful charger: "A *super*, super car but testing and winning races are different things. I didn't often have to wring Bertha's neck and drive her to the limit, but when I did it was just a question of working away, persisting, as you would in any racing car".

Motor took advantage of the track test opportunity to check the performance offered by *Baby Bertha* with their sophisticated fifth wheel. Gerry Marshall completed the acceleration runs for them, recording: 0-60mph in 4.2 seconds; 0-100mph in 7.8 seconds and 0-120mph in 12 seconds. For comparison the same magazine quoted 0-60mph in 5.1 seconds for DTV's 2-litre racing Viva GT (0-100mph in 14 seconds) and the fabled Lamborghini Countach's 0-100 time of 12.1 seconds, the latter always claimed to be the fastest production car in the world.

Some Baby!

It wasn't
only Vauxhalls ...

Just as it was ironic that Gerry's most significant international win should come with the almost obsolete Magnum coupé, at a time when the Chevette's rally performances were pointing the way to an emphasis on the bumpy bits for DTV, so it was also ironic that two of his best known results came with a four letter word. That's about the impact dropping the Ford name has with some of General Motors' Kings and Princes! As Gerry has said "Ford really was a four-letter word to us through most of my racing days at DTV. I spent literally hours testing, practising and racing, just trying to beat whatever kind of device they were backing. Still, on two occasions the Ford Escort was to prove a turning point in my career".

The 1971 season was to be dominated by a new talking point on the saloon car front. Ford had introduced the clever idea of showing off their (almost) standard products at a number of one-off celebrity races at their FordSport days. They now took the point a bit further by dint of jointly promoting Britain's first one-marque championship for what were meant to be production saloons (Ford Escort Mexicos) on racing rubber. The BRSCC organised the twelve-round Castrol/Mexico Challenge Series superbly, but Ford's sporting hierarchy had two fabulous jokers up their sleeves to induce white-hot competition. First they slapped in a hefty scale of rewards, culminating in the then-new Cosworth-BDA engine Escort RS1600 road car as first prize. Then, with a chuckle and the hearty connivance of some Islington residents who knew their overseas racing, they introduced the character Gerry now describes: "I thought he was a wild man. No car control: he kept falling off. He didn't do *a race* without a spin or a roll, either in the race, or in practice ... but he was a *goer*! Everybody else says they could see the qualities that took him into Formula 1, but I couldn't, I was wrong, but that was my opinion at the time".

The "wild man" was South Africa's Jody Scheckter. Driving a Castrol-striped Escort to destruction with the rest of the 1.6 litre pack, the young man who was to literally set the aces talking on future occasions in F1, arrived in Britain to drive Formula Ford and be a star. All of which he did, but Ford men and commentator/journalist Andrew Marriott (who was absolutely sold on Jody's future and knew his prowess in a saloon at home) also made the curly headed immigrant entertain us in a saloon too. Jody didn't think a lot of the cars - which had about 80-horsepower at the rear wheels and rarely exceeded 100mph when racing - but he always put on a show. Sideways, two, three, or even four wheels off the ground, Jody became the man to beat in Mexico racing, simply because Ford were interested in his future.

Oddly enough the man to win the championship that year had no Ford affiliations, and he had temporarily fallen out with Castrol too! Mr. Marshall was determined to show both Ford and Castrol what he was capable of. The eventual result was the Golden Esso Uniflo can colour-scheme Mexico he drove to win the title. It was a long, and often controversial, fight, for besides the obvious Marshall *v* Scheckter show (and one marque racing has never seen such a confrontation) there were Barrie Williams and Rod Mansfield to contend with as well, both of them absolute top-notch drivers in these cars. By coincidence it was also the year that now-Vauxhall rally star Chris Sclater was out in the Mexico menagerie too.

How did Marshall get involved in Mexicos? "I went up to the first round, which was at Rufforth with a friend (Alan Keefe) who was competing in one of the Escorts. I got talking with Larry Sevitt, an old friend from the days when Bill McGovern and I started road racing together. Sevitt had a full Abarth 850TC saloon, a very fast car. He subsequently bought a Mini and raced that too, though his enthusiasm always got the better of his car control! Anyway, he was now an owner of Tiran Auto Centre in Willesden and had a Mexico for the championship, prepared by an excellent mechanic, Keith Tillbrook. The idea was that either he or Bill McGovern would drive it, but Bill was warned off by Des O'Dell up at Chrysler (McGovern was then set for a series of saloon car titles with Bevan-modified Imps).

"Larry drove it at that first meeting and spun off at every possible opportunity he could find. After that he asked me to drive it at the next meeting, which was at Snetterton. We went testing during the week at that track. John Miles was up there in Jeff Uren's car. We did a 2 minutes dead lap, 2.9 seconds faster than Miles in the Uren car, and our Mexico was pulling 5600rpm in top: Jeff himself was also there, and a lot slower than Miles, so they obviously hadn't got that car quite right. I did drive it the following season and it was a winning car then.

"That was on the Thursday. For the Sunday race at Snett we again got a lap in 2 minutes dead, a new record, and I won after a big dice with Squeaker (Barrie Williams) and Rod Mansfield. After, I went to see Roger Willis at Castrol and told him I thought I was going to win this Mexico series and how about some support? Especially as the Vauxhalls were using their oil. Roger said: 'Not interested. We have this South-African fella called Scheckter who's going to win'. Dear old Roger, even in those days he was totally loyal to Stuart Turner and the Ford Motor Co ... that's what made me so determined to get a rival oil company and beat Jody!"

Throughout the season there were to be some epic dices as Marshall strove to make his point, winning races and taking two records to win the title after a victory in the final round at Brands Hatch.

Gerry had driven the car in fine style all year, showed that he wasn't afraid of the closest possible racing (the club racing Vauxhalls were now taken a lot more seriously, leading to accusations of DTV overkill already!) and he had made his message clear to Castrol! Indirectly the point could not escape them - or Ford Competition UK boss Stuart Turner, for he had to give Gerry the first Mexico-title and the car. Still, Stuart's image - he was nicknamed simply 'God' inside Ford - was reinforced by Scheckter's subsequent record. Gerry recalls Oulton Park as his best race in the series: "I outbraked Jody at Esso and won. Turner gave Scheckter a bollocking afterwards!" Ah, yes, the car. Gerry M. did not take the RS1600, he prevailed on the powers at Ford to let him have a Zodiac Executive which never did seem to carry the correct registration.

The other Escort adventure was the 1974 Texaco Tour of Britain. "That year Vauxhall said to me 'You are a racing driver and drive racing cars. The Tour of Britain is for rally drivers and they shall drive our cars'. This followed my super accident in 1973 while attempting to learn a little more about rallying in Coburn's rebuild of my original old Group 1 car (referred to earlier).

"That was why I did not do the Tour in 1973, as Vauxhall's threw a small fit of pique! Having seen the Tour in 1973 I decided that was an event I really *must* do. I asked Vauxhall and got much the same answer, so I said fair enough ... Possibly I led them to believe that I might be doing it in another Vauxhall. In fact I put some money into, and entered, Tim Stock's car.

"I asked if I could have a release from my contract (which was only put into written

Monsieur Paul Roget of Champagne fame and myself discuss the merits of his product as 'Doris' Craft looks on: Clive Richardson, who accompanied me on this light-hearted 'road-race' to France in 1976 has obviously passed out somewhere ...

form after his 1971 Mexico racing exploits!) for the event. They readily agreed, though I think they still thought I was going to do it in a Vauxhall. I spoke to Tony Mason - Ford's rally manager at the time - at Brands Hatch. He passed on the thought of my driving for Ford on the Tour to Stuart Turner, and he thought it was a marvellous idea.

"Originally it was going to be a three-car team of myself, Roger Clark and Timo Makinen. However the sponsorship fell down, so it was just Roger Clark and myself entered by the Ford Motor Company. A turning point in my career, and in that of my co-driver for the event, Paul White, because it was his first ever Ford works ride. You could say he never looked back ... but I'm not sure if that's accurate as he now works for Chrysler Competitions!

"In retaliation - although it was always denied as such - Vauxhall then got James Hunt to drive for them. A strange situation: James Hunt normally drove a Ford-engined Hesketh and was out in the Vauxhall ... then there's a Vauxhall contracted driver out in a Ford: quite laughable".

The Fords were prepared in something of a hurry between the company's normally hectic rallying and racing commitments. They were a pair of identical white Escort RS2000s, complete with the strange standard blue stripes uncertainly positioned halfway up their sides, and prepared to a last-minute homologation of twin Solex carburettors for Group 1. This woke the lethargic ex-Cortina 2-litre engines up considerably and made the RS2000 into a competitive proposition, for the braking and handling was already the subject of eulogistic comment from both Marshall and Clark.

Right up to the last minutes of scrutineering on Thursday afternoon it looked as though Ford were not going to get the cars ready in time. When the cars eventually did arrive - equipped with 4:1 final drives in place of the planned 3.7:1 that day - the hard- *115*

I have driven in three Spa 24 Hour races. This is 1976 when Tony Lanfranchi and I shared the car and it stopped 1.5 hours from the finish. Still, it was good for a good skid, as Alan Foster might say! *Courtesy J. St. J. Bloxham.*

This proves both Peter Brock and I drive over kerbs in long races: it could be either of us! Tourist Trophy 1976, the year this car won its class in the RAC Championship.

Tony Lanfranchi and I have spent quite a few draughty moments at Brands ... *Courtesy J. St. J. Bloxham.*

Dick (left) and Geoff still seem overawed by the size of Baby Bertha's tubes! *Courtesy Colin Taylor.*

It wasn't only Vauxhalls ...

We entered a Libre race at Brands for a giggle. Here I give Phillip Guerola's March a frightening spectacle in the mirrors before passing to win!

pressed mechanics and a sweaty Ford Public Relations man walked them through the assembled experts. Instead of formal papers, they had the aid only of a short telex message from the CSI in Paris, assuring the British Authorities that the car's homologation papers had been passed, and that it was legal for competition!

In 1974 the Tour was once again sponsored by the Avon Tyre concern, as it had been in 1973 when James Hunt won. For 1974 the organisers put in a little more loose surface motoring and the challenge of the Mynedd Eppynt army range roads. Clark and Marshall had only settled on the steel braced Dunlop SP4 tyres at a test session shortly before the event - Avon 'control' tyres proved better than other more sporting Dunlop designs, but the SP4 Dunlop (designed for tyre life!) proved just the job for the 140-horsepower light Fords.

The first race track confrontation on the event was at Mallory Park. Conditions were dry and I was sitting with the DTV crowd, Messrs Marshall and Clark having sauntered off toward their cars, Gerry still wearing his DTV teeshirt under his overalls to the considerable consternation of the Ford staff. When Gerry gave them 'a quick flash' you would have thought he represented a brigade of perverts from the horror revealed on their faces.

Chris Coburn was at that time running the DTV operation and the Vauxhall Magnums. Before the start Chris was ribbing some of the Ford people about the large margin he expected the Magnums to thrash the Escorts by, especially on the track, where the Vauxhalls were more powerful, and looked better equipped with wider wheels and tyres. As Gerry says now: "After we had done that last-minute tyre testing I met with Lanfranchi and Clark at the Bull at Barton Mills. We had two half-glasses of shandy - assuming we have a large police readership for motor racing biographies - and an orange juice.

We all decided that the man to win was going to be Gordon Spice (Capri 3-litre) or

Showbusiness: Bertha and I add a touch of class to a Copenhagen display.

Andrew Cowan in the Vauxhall. A week later, there we were, the three of us: Clark, second, by only eighteen seconds, Marshall, and third Lanfranchi, with that big BMW!

Even Coburn's mobile face was unable to register suitable amazement when the two striped Escorts simply motored away from everyone at Mallory. As the two Escorts established an ever greater margin of supremacy at the front, Ford had a new worry about the Clark/Marshall act, fondly nick-named: Écurie Beer-Gut". That problem was a public one, Clark and Marshall were driving the Escorts inches apart at almost any angle, on any line, as they swept round. Clark's position at Ford as Britain's number 1 rally driver had been earned by sheer fighting spirit, and he wasn't about to let any cissy racing driver past. Roger had raced on quite a few occasions previously, but he found his track knowledge sadly lacking throughout the event (except at Oulton Park, where he was significantly smoother) and so he would simply arrive at any given corner before Marshall, by hook or by crook, and turn the car at right angles to go through! Gerry would be tucked in tight behind - occasionally bouncing through the rough in his efforts to see that he didn't touch the Ford man.

When Peter Ashcroft, the Ford Boreham manager today, saw the two at play at Mallory he managed a weak smile and confirmed that he *still* would not be giving team orders. "The daft buggers can sort it out themselves", he said in best dour Lancashire dialect before a huge grin swept over his features. There had been the awful memory of the works Capris' appearances on the previous year's Tour to erase, and the little white and blue Escorts had done that with honour.

Over the long weekend of July sport that made up the Avon Motor Tour of Britain 1974, the Clark/Marshall circuit show drew all the attention. From start to finish no quarter was given between the pairing as they hurtled round Oulton Park in Cheshire, Silverstone in Northamptonshire, Cadwell Park in Lincolnshire, and even around Snet- *119* terton in Norfolk at night. In the dark their proximity at up to 120mph was frightening. Because the rear windows were heavily taped to prevent the drivers being blinded by pursuing lights it was hard to see what was going on. Today Marshall is still unimpressed by the story that Roger switched his lights out to sneak past ahead at the finish: "The object was just to get Clark round as fast as possible, my position was irrelevant on the Tour. Time was all that mattered", Marshall says stoically. In fact hundreds of people were riveted by the sight of the two Escorts hurtling out of the night winking lights, or on at least one occasion, with the headlamps firmly off on one car as they contested the lead. The fact remains that Clark was determined to win at all costs, and Marshall was the 'guest' driver, but no contracted Ford pilot has ever backed up his team leader with quite the skilful devotion Marshall exhibited that weekend.

Back in Birmingham, the celebrations at the Post House Hotel on the Sunday night were, in a word, thorough. In other words the police were in attendance by the small hours, though by that time even Messrs Clark and Marshall were not in the mischief that one might expect from two such strong personalities after a crushing text-book victory. Gerry, "... enjoyed the whole event. I liked the way the Ford people left you alone to get on with the job. I think a lot of them thought I might be handy on the circuits but just thought the loose was a question of, at best, my falling off gently!" As Clark confirmed, the close racing stuff had all been much more fraught to watch than it seemed to Clark and Marshall: neither car was marked at the end from contact damage, though they both had fair imitations of sand blasting from the perpetual tight slipstreaming, on and frequently off, the track!

Those two Ford escapades were valuable in convincing Vauxhall about Gerry's serious intentions on different occasions. They are perhaps the best-known examples of his driving outside Vauxhall during the decade he spent mainly with the Luton marque, but there were a lot more marques in Gerry's life during those Vauxhall years as well, as you will see in *Marshall's Marque Miscellany*, or the next chapter, as it might otherwise be known.

From Lister-Jaguar to Formula Ford ...and back

"Would you like to drive it?" That invitation must have been extended to Gerry Marshall on literally thousands of occasions. Sometimes, as in the case of a Mercedes 300SL, the invitation would be forthcoming after earnest chat from Marshall's persuasive tongue, but far more usually his curiosity, and the desire of an owner/potential vendor to find out more will lead to an impromptu session. Gerry has taken such test drives under all conditions from the science fiction secrets of General Motors' computer-equipped laboratories to a rainy day on the nearest section of British carriageway. Either way his opinions are pungent, often hilarious and always individual. I have never met anyone who has driven such a large number of cars, and carried out a successful competition career associated predominantly with one marque. His appetite for new machinery, road or competition, really is insatiable. As a trader he has an advantage over most, of course, but he has always tried to keep a stable of his own cars as well. By far the largest soft spot - and when Gerry has a soft spot it is bigger than life, as usual - has been and still is for Jaguars. Mainly the saloon models of the late fifties and early sixties (3.4 and 3.8-litres) plus the occasional E-type. Today he still has a superb 3.4 that was scheduled for delivery to Mike Hawthorn before that Englishman died in 1959. Naturally the other marque to feature in large numbers in his memories is Vauxhall, and this looks to be a trait that will stay with him well into the years after the expiry of his racing contract. Here we look at some of the cars that Gerry drove, predominantly while he was "... that chap who races a Vauxhall", but to get a Mercedes (a classic at that) into the book I'll start with an exception from long before his Vauxhall days ...

"It was while I was working at Dealer's Deliveries. An American and his wife appeared, complete with a 300 SL Roadster which had a specially tuned engine. He had picked it up from Stuttgart himself and he wanted to see the driver who was going to take it down to the docks for shipping: not surprisingly he wasn't going to trust anyone with this car.

"He brought the car to the office ... saw all the drivers we had got there and, not surprisingly, wasn't too keen to let anyone out in it! I got chatting to him - I must have been all of eighteen at the time - somehow or other he was foolish enough to let me take this thing to the docks. It was only to one of the London docks, but it meant I had the car overnight: a road-modified 300SL which I believe was identical to the one Rob Walker had at the time. A super car, so bloody fast, and there's me, an eighteen-year-old accident driving it. A beautiful car, and one I'd love to drive again now ... I don't know who was more relieved about my getting it to the docks safely, but everyone from the boss to myself must have let out a mighty sigh when the car did go onboard unscratched!"

Although it did not produce much in the way of results, a competition meeting with another American produced Gerry's first forays into Europe. Rexford Finnegan was in the American airforce but serving, and racing a 1275 Mini-Cooper 'S', in Britain. Gerry

121

'Albert' Clark and I getting ourselves noticed at the Doghouse Ball in London. *Courtesy Simone Grant.*

Bill Blydenstein, Carol Marshall, Gerry and Will Sparrow at the Motor Show. Gerry is actually saying to Will: "If Bill keeps Carol talking we can nip over and see the bird on the TVR stand!" *Courtesy Colin Taylor.*

Drinking is not my scene really, but I'd better help the organisers out ... *Courtesy Colin Taylor.*

"Deep Throat" was nothing like this! Filming with John Mills (right).

What might have been, if I'd been born ten years ealier! Aged Jaguar is ill-treated by large man, an obvious case for the RSPCA! Taken at Silverstone in March 1977 during a winning run. *Courtesy John Gaisford.*

met Finnegan at Snetterton in 1967, when Marshall managed to persuade the USAAF Major to allow Marshall to drive his Mini as a co-driver in the annual 500Km race. The partnership got off to a reasonable start, Gerry was certainly impressed by the American's straight-laced courtesy while Finnegan could see from a comparison of his lap times that Gerry was worth employing. In the race itself the Mini retired while eleventh, but Finnegan had mentioned to Marshall that there was the possibility of going racing in the following year's European Touring Car Championship series. Would Marshall be interested?

Interested ... He was ecstatic! A chance to see all the places he had been reading about so assiduously over the years, you bet Gerry would accompany him. They towed down to Monza in Northern Italy in style, using Finnegan's Mustang. "That was a little bit flash", Gerry recalls. "Here I was, off to my first race in Europe, and rolling along in a big blue Mustang. It was a super weekend, though there was no result to speak of. At that time we were racing under Group 5, which was just a confusing name for Group 2, and I remember the Cooper Car Co. had all their Mini aces of the day down there - Rhodes, Hopkirk and so on. They were running fuel injection and eight-port heads, which Ginger Devlin had a real job convincing the Italian authorities were legal. This didn't affect us though, we just had a single 45DCOE Weber on a car built by Blydenstein. The car was good, but we suffered this overheating problem. We did a head gasket in the end, but I had a super start to the race. I was keeping up with Rhodes in the works Mini - in retrospect I now realise that I was trying and he wasn't! It was a six-hour race after all..."

Their next, and final as it was to turn out, ETCC foray was to the Nürburgring. Even now Marshall has never raced there again, "but I would still rate it as my second favourite in Europe: only Spa's better than that". The trip did not produce a finish - Finnegan put the car off at the beginning of his stint - but it did produce more than its share of anec-

Here I am overtaking Ronnie Peterson's Jägermeister BMW on the outside! Or could it be that his 320i is overtaking my Group 1 car? Tony Lanfranchi, Barrie Williams and I hired this Group 1 3-litre Si jointly and had a very enjoyable outing in the 1977 Silverstone 6 Hours. *Courtesy Colin Taylor.*

dotes, especially about practice. The first incident was fairly straightforward:"I borrowed John Fitzpatrick's Lotus Cortina, promised to take it very easy, and disappeared out for a couple of laps. What I didn't know was that Ralph Broad, John's mentor of course, and one of the entrants for Ford Motor Co. Escorts at this event, was watching at *Adenau Forst*. Ralph duly came back to John with the story that the Cortina was getting very sideways in that nasty rally driver Roger Clark's hands ... it wasn't Roger at all, it was me! John has forgiven me since and talks to me, which is more than you can say for Gordon Spice, who I beat in a running race bet that weekend. I don't think I was ever forgiven for that!"

The feature of practice was: "We hired a Renault R10–which was an R8 with an extra wart up front! It was on narrow bicycle rim Michelin Xs: the only reason neither Rex nor I did not write the thing off was that we were both so bloody frightened of it the whole time. That car frightened me far more than any racing car has before or since!" Gerry did have one golden opportunity to learn the circuit properly though and that was a ride with David Hobbs in a Mercedes road car - "These were the halcyon days of sports car racing with all the Porsches, GT40s and even the Ford P3L project. In fact it was only weeks after Chris Irwin's terrible accident. Hobbs impressed me very much with how a professional driver should behave. We were really going in the Mercedes, but he was so smooth and in control ... I can still remember most of the instructions he gave me that day".

The Mini was quite badly damaged by the owner's excursion and that was the end of Marshall's Mini racing days in Europe. He has continued to drive the model in Britain on occasion. The outing he recalls with most pride, but more sorrow, was in 1970 at Mallory Park on Boxing Day. "I was driving the ex-Rob Mason 1000cc Mini Group 2 car, then owned by Robbie Gordon. Against me was that fabulous 1-litre Anglia driven by a man I really did respect in saloon cars, and one of the very, very few to make it into F1 from an Anglia - Roger Williamson. Anyway, I also put in a rare performance that day, *125*

Old and new, Colin Vandervell and I play at Brands: in 1978 I took over his Capri, seen here just leading my DTV Magnum.

Beautiful Basil and the beast. Van Rooyen and I with the Hardie Ferodo Holden before the 1977 Bathurst event. A disappointing outing.

because I actually managed to beat Roger on his home circuit: I think that may have been the only time he and his Anglia were ever beaten fair and square". Roger went on to greater things in Formula cars of course, the partnership with Tom Wheatcroft creating a British combination that really did look set for the pinnacles of Formula 1 until Roger died in a dreadful fiery accident at Zandvoort. A tragedy emphasised because of David Purley's sheer courage (that earned him an MBE of course) in trying to remove the young Leicestershire man from his burning March. As Gerry aptly put it: "He was a smashing bloke in saloons and just as cheerful when he started climbing to the top. A lovely grin, but a real hard competitor". Today Marshall and Donington circuit owner Wheatcroft remain such good friends that Marshall's name is permanently linked with that of a circuit drinks establishment.

Another marque from his early days re-appears during Marshall's reign at DTV – Lotus. "Graham Arnold, then the marketing director of Lotus, has been a good friend of mine for many years. He is always one to see a bit of publicity and the idea was to build me a Lotus 7 *with an FVA Formula 2 engine*. It would have promoted Lotus components and vehicles, complete with a bloody great wing and a five-speed gearbox. This all took so long to come about that, hearing the times I had been doing in the Brands Hatch Formula Ford school cars, they built me an FF Lotus 61. It was slightly wider than normal (designated 61L for large!) and the idea was that Mike Spence Ltd. would run it.

"That company was unable to run it - it was too soon after Mike himself was killed at Indianapolis - so Victor Raysbrook, another old acquaintance in Watford, his Lotus dealership took the job on. We did the first race at Snetterton and I was dicing merrily along in second place. Last lap, last corner and the gearlever came off in my hand, which was a pity. A pity because it was a really enjoyable little thing to drive, complete with its Holbay engine, but in the next, and to date my only further FF race, it staggered from disaster to disaster: Vic really didn't have the right racing set-up to back up the car, and I spent my racing time avoiding other people's accidents! We had some seconds and thirds, but most of the time I tried to avoid the normal FF practice of driving into people, it's just not dignified at my time of life.

"I liked FF to drive - provided I was a long way away from the other lunatics and assorted hooligans. This was in the days of the Firestone F100 tyres and the cars were lovely to drive without traffic. I remember once being on the front row of the grid at Mallory, alongside Dave Walker (who briefly appeared as one of the chain of Lotus GP drivers) but I gave it up after a Snetterton first corner incident. We went off the line, just before the first corner the row in front of me all hit each other. I lifted off and everyone else ran over the top of us! I had actually put my hand up to show everyone behind what was happening, it was so obvious they were going to hit each other. For a married man with two children, forget it!"

Other racing appearances in single seaters were not forthcoming, though Marshall nearly did appear in Alan Fraser's Lola F5000 car at Oulton Park. Gerry had driven one of Alan's fabulous Fraser-Imps, but was let down just before a good finish. That would have been for the Gold Cup, when Lanfranchi had his terrible road accident in 1969. The big V8-engined cars seemed ideal for Gerry's style but it was not to be, "... which was probably just as well", as Gerry says today. Other appearances in Lotus were on the cards though, for he got together with Victor Raysbrook again in an Elan starting in 1972. Though the pairing produced the fastest practice times, finishes were non-existent. It was left to subsequent driver John 'Plastic' Pearson to really get to grips with the car's preparation and score a lot of success with the smart white and blue Lotus.

Through his love for Jaguars Gerry also made a piece of circuit history. In 1972 he could be seen driving the Hexagon of Highgate Lister-Jaguar to victory in the last event held at Crystal Palace South London parkland. "Paul Michaels at Hexagon reckoned he owed me a drive. I had already had a go at their Birdcage Maserati at a Silverstone round of the JCB Championship. Then we had been racing on the Grand Prix circuit and Nick

Faure had been racing their Lister-Jaguar. Unfortunately what looked like being a super race was spoilt for me when, on the first lap at Stowe, Faure spun the Lister. I went off line to avoid him, but in doing so I spun myself, denting the back of the car and putting myself out of the race.

"Michaels then let me drive again, but this time in the Lister at Crystal Palace. Believe it or not we came in second in class against *modern* cars, so it was quite a good outing. I thoroughly enjoyed this car - which had a space-frame chassis and had been converted from a coupé body back to normal open style by Hexagon, putting it back to the condition it had been in when Bruce Halford had last won a race with it in the early 1960s. Then I was offered the chance to take the Lister (which had originally performed in Lumsden and Sargent's hands at Le Mans) out in the last meeting at the Palace. Nick Faure was there as Hexagon's number 1 man - he'd been with them for several seasons at that stage—and he chose to drive the Birdcage Maserati while I had the Lister again.

"We were against such notables as Richard Bond (ex-Jim Clark Lister-Jaguar) and *the* ace in the series, Willie Green (who drove for the series sponsors). We had a super race, it really was a tight one—but I just managed to hang on and win the very last race on the circuit. So that's one bit of racing history that cannot be taken away from me.

"I subsequently bought a Lister of my own. In fact the car, driven by Dick Tindell, was in that Crystal Palace race. The Hexagon car had two problems. First, the engine wasn't smooth enough at the top end: it was hardly worth going beyond 5500rpm. The second was that it had great big Can-Am brakes on it and they grabbed, locking the right-hand front wheel the whole time. It was a lovely handling car, but the first time I ever drove it I had a big scare with it. I was up at Silverstone and it lost one of the wheels, which they had just had rebuilt! Luckily no damage done, but it was a fright alright as it was only a week or so after I had lost the wheel *for the second time* in the Vauxhalls! So I lost three wheels in three weeks in all. Fortunately the Jaguar one came off just as I was coming out of Becketts at about 60mph, so I could steer it to a stop without any damage." Casting back to his TVR days, when lost wheels became almost routine, it seems Marshall's true vocation was to be a tricyclist!

"Incidentally, I also drove Hexagon's GT40 while I was up there. It had always been an ambition of mine to drive a GT40 ... and it was every bit as lovely as I thought it would be. The straightline stability was an absolute revelation ...". A slightly more obscure piece of motoring history came Gerry's way at Thruxton in 1971. Renewing his acquaintance with designer Frank Costin, Gerry drove the unique Costin Amigo sports racer to a tidy fourth overall, winner of the 2-litre class after a last-lap dash past Alister Cowin's Chevron. A rare victory for a rare machine. Gerry recalls, with the aid of his diary, that it managed to lap in 1 minute 30 seconds, which now would be a good time for a production saloon like a Dolomite or 3-litre Capri, which shows how fast things have moved in the seventies.

At various stages in his association with General Motors Marshall obviously attracted the accolade of being one competition human being they could thoroughly trust. When the Ventora was due to have 4.2 or 4.7-litre automatic V8s in the roadgoing version, which the racing Ventora was intended to promote, Marshall drove the prototypes. Now all this work in England was fair enough, but the ultimate call for his presence, and a glimpse inside General Motors, came in a letter dated June 14, 1974 and headed with the address of the GM Technical Centre at Warren in Michigan.

It said: "Dear Gerry, Just a short note to let you know that our whole organization has been enthusiastically following your successful races. The new Firenza and the big Ventora V8 are especially exciting vehicles.

"If it is at all possible, I would like to have you come over and visit us here at the Tech Center ..." There followed a few details, and it was signed Bill (William L. Mitchell). At that time this was the equivalent of having the Pope ask you in for a social chat, for Mitchell was perhaps the most powerful influence on car design in the world, as he headed up the biggest design operation in the world for the producers of the largest number of cars.

Of course Gerry did go, "... and had a fabulous time for a couple of weeks. There were a lot of things that I would not discuss even now, even though Bill has retired, but the highlight was having his personal fleet of prototypes at my disposal. There were all sorts of weird and wonderful combinations to try, and Corvettes busting out of my ears. Even so, I had one driving regret. I was due to race the space frame Stingray race car. Literally the only one in the world and it was scheduled to make an appearance at Watkins Glen in a special twenty-five year commemorative race for the circuit. At the last moment it was decided to abort, which was bit of a shame as it must have been the most accelerative car I ever drove. I tried it at the company's proving ground and it really was something else.

Another ambition that was fulfilled, but in a rather different manner to that originally intended, had been the chance of winning races in a Jaguar saloon. Gerry was brought up on the heroic deeds of people like Salvadori, Moss and Hawthorn. When they could be inveigled into racing versions of the Jaguar saloons, Gerry and thousands of others would watch wide-eyed at the incredible antics as these top-liners fought to extract abilities that even Jaguar's engineering department barely foresaw as being necessary in what was then the epitome of sporting motoring for the family man.

Literally it was nearly twenty years after such sights had gladdened the spectators' hearts that a series called Classic Saloon Car Racing began to make an impact on the British Club scene, and Gerry was involved both as an entrant and driver wherever he could be. This means that he has now driven a lot of machinery he lusted after as a youth, including Jaguars. However the model that he has twice won with, setting new records - Craig Hinton's 2.4-litre saloon - was not quite the same bombshell as the later 3.8 models. If those capacities are eventually let in, doubtless Gerry will be one of the first to join in.

BMWs have figured in the Marshall career too. In 1973 he did some testing and in a race at Brands Hatch in a 3.0Si finished third in the BMW Concessionaires car. He did not drive that car again, owing to his contractual obligations at Vauxhall, but he did enjoy an hilarious ride in another 3.0Si at Silverstone. Barrie Williams, Tony Lanfranchi and Gerry each put up £250 and drove the BMW 3.0Si belonging to Monorep in the 1977 Six Hours World Championship round. This contained the cream of the exotic Group 5 Porsches and BMWs which so expensively contested this so-called 'Silhouette Series'. The BMW was not going to win any prizes - only the author had the necessary lack of talent and machinery to qualify any slower!–but the terrible trio certainly enjoyed slinging the poor fat saloon into ever greater slides in clouds of blue smoke. Williams remembers: "There was a dent on the bonnet after Gerry's practice - he had *hit* a *Porsche* up the back! I mean, who else could find a turbo-Porsche in mid-corner and hit it up the arse? Apparently it was all nothing to do with Gerry, the other bloke just got in the way!

"We had an unbelievable driver's meeting to sort out our 'tactics'; mainly whose round it was ... Tony and I decided Gerry could cause more carnage in the first few laps, based on practice, so we let him go first. After three laps of the race he failed to appear. So we set off to search for him, fearing the worst. There he was, stranded by the electrics on the circuit, this huge figure with an *immense* crowd gathered round, offering advice. When we had fixed the blown fuse it took all of us ten minutes to buckle him up again and send him on his way". As expected they didn't win any prizes, but the car was still running at the finish, with the 'terrible trio's' tales echoing through the Silverstone Clubhouse for many happy hours that night. Real club racing!

A couple of foreign trips to drive General Motors cars - an Opel at Spa for the 1972 Twenty-four Hour Race, and a Holden Torana for 1977s Bathurst based Hardie Ferodo 1000 in Australia - resulted in major upsets. The Opel "... was the best-sounding car I ever drove: it was a 2.8 Commodore with the wrong camshafts in. This made it rev to

So would you want to get out! The "Bugsey Malone" film car gets the treatment from Brian 'Slim' Atthews (standing), Jock Robertson (attempting to steer) and Barrie Williams, pushing. *Courtesy J. St. J. Bloxham.*

about 8000, when the straight-six sounded absolutely *fabulous*. The only trouble was that it only did a couple of hours in the Twenty-four Hours before it dropped its bloody propshaft, right in the middle of the Masta Kink, in the pouring rain. Not only was it the best noise, but also the fastest-cursed car in my life!"

The trip down under was "... one of my biggest racing disappointments. I had been invited by Bill Patterson Racing to drive a Holden Torana, which I shared with Basil van Rooyen. The Holden Torana is about the size of an Opel Ascona, but with a 380bhp 5-litre V8 engine, the same as the one which was the base for the Repco-Holden V8 in Baby Bertha. Unfortunately our car suffered from a lack of preparation, and we qualified about eighteenth on the grid - even so we were clocked on Conrod Straight at 161mph! I discovered why it had been called Conrod Straight after five of the scheduled seven hours or so racing, the Torana throwing a connecting rod in a *big* way".

So far as the race itself was concerned Gerry made the following observations in *Autosport*: "Everyone but everyone knows about it ... it's as big a talking point as Elsie Tanner being pregnant ... in Australia you work *up* to saloons ... the first corner after the start is a lefthander called Hell Corner, which does nothing for your confidence, and round the back on the downhill stretch, the drops are just fantastic. Where there are steep earth banks (and spectators) on the right, and sheer drops on the left, they put Armco in front of the spectators. Jacky Ickx said he thought it was on the wrong side".

An unhappy car, but one that I will mention among many that have to be omitted, was a Chrysler Avenger. Purchased from Peter Slade it was pressed into competition at Thruxton and came home with a new record and a class victory. "Flushed with this success, I entered it the following weekend at Brands Hatch. Fortunately I had insured it with dear old Ian Bracey ('Baked Bean' to some) who paid up like a gent ... In the race I   *131* made a super start and was lying about third or fourth overall when, on the top straight, of all places, I got knocked off by a wayward Camaro, which was driving its owner!'' Chrysler has never been lucky for Gerry and that car was a dramatic end to any further association with the marque.

He has driven many more saloons than I can mention: "I have even *skidded* a Marina", he will tell you with mock pride, but we have to stop somewhere. One thing's for sure, he has always been the central saloon attraction, whatever the marque.

From the past to the more recent past, what happened to Marshall after the Vauxhall contract expired? At first he was very dispirited and talked frequently, if probably not seriously, of giving up altogether, even placing some ads that said pretty rude things about production saloon car racing within the closing pages of *Autosport*. Previously his advertising had always been noted for the rude congratulatory PS messages, now it seemed it was all over.

There was a bit of a false start with a Sussex entrepreneur who announced that G. Marshall would be driving a 3-litre Capri all over Europe. This message went out to the Press just before Christmas 1977 and effectively left many thinking "Marshall's alright, we'll see him again in '78". Unfortunately this was far from the case and Gerry had to work very hard to put any sort of deals together for this critical period after the DTV contract was terminated.

Typically he came up with two deals. The first was to run a Downie Racing prepared Dolomite Sprint in the production saloon car series, and the second was to take over Colin Vandervell's 3-litre Capri and campaign that in the national saloon car championship. The Dolomite was beautifully prepared by the group who comprise Downie, people whose names are not unfamiliar for the development work at the Triumph Engineering department in some cases! Although the car carried Castrol sponsorship, that was really to avoid "...racing like a bald chicken I mean a racing car has to have stickers, doesn't it..." Thus spoke Gerry of a project that really represented his own cash initially. The Capri raced on under Triplex sponsorship (as did the Dolomite after it had shown Championship-leading form) but, as ever in racing, the money was not expected to be enough. Luckily Marshall had got used to sponsoring other people in the sport and putting some of his own money in, otherwise the shock could have been too much for him after ten years of racing (mainly) at someone else's expense.

Also typical were the entertaining and successful performances he put in driving these cars. His great experience had included other examples of both Dolomite and Capri before. He first raced a Capri, from Boreham, on an experimental basis for a 1971 handicap race at Brands Hatch. The Dolomite Sprint of Bob Saunders was also raced by Gerry in 1976. Although his own 1978 Dolomite was in the smaller 2.5-litre division of its series, it was not long before Gerry had chalked up an outright victory with the car (at Thruxton) and he was not that far off winning in his first apearance with the Capri. That was a vintage Marshall performance too. The occasion was the opening round of the 1978 Tricentol RAC Saloon Car Championship and Gerry was in amongst a pack of Capris; though they were dominated by Tony Dron's works Dolomite Sprint. Imagine the scene just before the race, the familiar Marshall figure can be seen taking the bracing air on the central runway. It is beginning to rain when a reporter approaches him: "'This should be good for you, weather like this, you'll kill them'', he says hopefully. Marshall (unmoved but beaming in his ample orange racer's kit). " – off! We've got the wrong type of wets. There's no chance, even a foolish motoring journalist can see that?'' Expounds at some length on the lack of testing time he's had in the Capri and the marvellous opposition. In the race, a supporter to the wet Daily Express Trophy, won by Keke Rosberg's Theodore (which tells you about the diabolical conditions), Marshall looms on the almost dripping TV monitors with great brio. The reporter, and many more inside the dryish island that is the Dunlop Tower at Silverstone, watch Dron pull away as predicted. Behind Marshall lays on a royal show to hold second place in the Ford, a second place that includes two

H.R.H. Prince Michael of Kent presented me with the prestigious ERA Trophy for my performance at Spa in the 1977 24 Hour race. Anthony Salmon of the BRDC stands between us, and looks almost as pleased at I was. *Courtesy Sound Stills Ltd.*

separate trips from the fastest lefthander on the circuit toward the final Woodcote complex, mainly by grass. Each time it seems that there is no way the pale blue and white Ford will ever regain the tarmac as it hurtles broadside along the surrounding verge toward the sturdy bridge supports before Woodcote. Each time, just like a magician, he saves his best trick for last and twitches the confused Capri 'back on the island'. For thousands of sodden spectators, appreciation of a fine show overcame the waves of water seeping from below and slashing down from the heavens.

So the end of Dealer Team Vauxhall in racing did not mean the end of our hero. Far from it, at the time of writing he was certainly enjoying more British success than he had since 1976. Only here for the Beer... More like only here for the cheer!

Cheer is a word Marshall knows quite a lot about. Aside from its obvious drinking connotations though, he has also come to mean cheer of a different sort to those who have had their competition bills paid by his efforts, including former Grand Prix World Champion Driver, Denis Hulme.

Sponsoring a World Champion ...and other tales

"A lot of people think that the *Mayfair* people were Tony Lanfranchi's sponsor, but they were not. Since they led me into the only deal in which *I* have sponsored a World Champion, even a former World Champion, perhaps it's a rather more interesting tale than most sponsorship stories", Marshall says in preparation of the background to the Tour of Britain 1976. Aside from driving for Vauxhall - that was the year of the James Hunt alarms and excursions all over Britain - Gerry had one Denis Hulme (yes that McLaren team Denis Hulme) driving an Opel for him.

How was the deal completed? "I had taken over the running of an Opel Commodore GS/E for Tony Lanfranchi in production racing. Tony originally had a sponsorship deal with a record company, but the cheques were not being honoured. I'll say they were not honoured - they bounced across the Atlantic! We had Monorep doing the actual transportation and fettling plus Broadspeed, subsequently Richard Longman, doing the engine. At first the car did not do very well, but I gave Tony an ultimatum and, in the proverbial manner, he went straight out and won the next race, which gave us all hope.

"Now I was looking for some more money to run this car, still in production saloon car racing. Through my solicitor, Howard Leftley, I came into contact with Fisk Publishing, and *Mayfair* magazine which belongs to his sister, who shelled out a couple of thousand quid to keep us going. They were only buying half a season. Still we had a nice thick coat of metalflake paint to hide all the dents and Tony was doing well. Then, halfway through the season, along come Peter Browning and Andrew Marriott on behalf of Texaco, wanting me to run Denis Hulme on the Tour that Texaco are to sponsor that year. A deal was put up, I got a few extra shillings from *Mayfair* and a few bob more from Texaco, and we were off.

"Monorep did all the service, Kleber supplied tyres and they even had Pete Lyons in along with Denny to write the story. I had enough problems of my own with the Vauxhalls that year, but everyone did a magnificent job and Denny came in tenth, winner of the production car class, in what had been a very tough rally-style event.

"Hulme turned out to be a really great, relaxed, guy. I still have a vision of him after the event, and the prizegiving, sitting by the pool at the Post House eyeing the girls along with everyone else.

"We had only one test session before the event with Denny. That was at Brands Hatch. We thought as he was an ex-World Champion he'd complain about everything and be a real misery, but the man who used to be called "The Bear" by the Press has really been tamed in retirement. You could not hope to meet a nicer guy. I'd love us to do another event with him".

In fact from 1974 to 1977 Gerry entered Marshal Wingfield Opel Commodore GS/Es that he says simply were; "the most successful Opels in racing. It was all done out of my own pocket, with assistance from *Mayfair* after the first two years. The drivers were Peter Hanson in 1974, Tony L 1975 and in 1976, and Jock Robertson for 1977. Quite honestly I thought the back-up from the Dealer Team in Britain was awful [there is a new

135

First there was Big Bertha, then Baby Bertha, so I suppose this was Megga Bertha! *Courtesy Vauxhall Motors.*

management now - J.W] and I would never want to sponsor an Opel again. Even when Jock won thousands in the Opel Cup series, we heard nothing from them: fine road cars, but they were obsolete for 1978, so I did not see any point in continuing. Tony did, and carried on with the *Mayfair* money, so that is where the confusion of sponsorship may have come from".

Jock Robertson was a significant name in Gerry's sponsorship activities. It has not always been a smooth relationship though, and when this was written the two were no longer linked. Gerry explained how Jock's career and the untimely death of John Wingfield (Marshall's business partner for many years, formally so from 1972 onwards) damaged their working relationship. "Jock worked for us at DTV in Shepreth as a mechanic. He built a Magnum up, a new car in which I saw him nearly beat Barrie Williams at Silverstone in 1974. I thought the lad was very good, he hadn't got a sponsor so I gave him a hand and entered his car for a bit .... I also wrote it off for him". That was the Snetterton multiple crash mentioned earlier but, "it was insured thank goodness, so were able to get it rebuilt and continue; in fact that car is still racing today, so far as I know.

"The following year I worked out that the car to have was the Mazda RX3, and it turned out I was right. I got a car from David Palmer at Mazda for a good price. Mathwall, a firm I have admired for many years, prepared it. Of course the car went on to win virtually every time out, and took both production saloon car championships, including the Radio 1, which was getting big publicity as Noel Edmonds was driving that year. Jock's a first class mechanic and a good driver, and the results spoke for themselves that year.

"The following year, unfortunately, he wanted to go single seater racing. I was not really very interested but I was inveigled into it by my late partner John. We thought we'd give Jock his head in single-seaters - but we had a disaster of the first order when we ordered the car. It came through late, without belts and several other bits and pieces, and I am still sueing them! Then we had to go for a Hawke, which was an excellent car, but Jock didn't seem to get on too well with the Formula Ford 2000. In the middle of all that my partner was killed [John Wingfield died at Thruxton in a racing accident. Tragically he was the second of two brothers to die on a circuit. Nevertheless their mother has continued to act in partnership with Gerry Marshall] so I was definitely very anti-single-seater racing. Thus it was a natural progression that Jock returned to saloon car racing for me in 1977. Even then he was not quite the same driver that I had watched in 1975, but then some change was, I suppose, inevitable."

In 1975 Jock Robertson also won mention in the Grovewood Awards, the prestigious annual presentations to drivers adjudged the most promising in the British Commonwealth.

None of Gerry's other sponsorships have brought those results since, but he sincerely does not do it for the glory. This can be seen by the fact that, time and time again, his money will go into the grass roots of the sport, making it possible for a driver to carry on (usually) saloon car racing in a quiet way. Often Gerry will drive a car he has backed, especially within the Classic Saloon Car series mentioned previously, but generally it's just a question of supporting proven friends and useful clubmen. "It is the only way to keep Lanfranchi and Williams in tax deductable drinking money", he says with mock resignation!

A day in the life of a super-enthusiast

The past is all very well, but what does life hold for Gerry Marshall today? It is no good trying to spend days with him looking out for some archetypal twenty-four hours that sums up his present existence, besides which his still-awesome enthusiasm does not really come to light until the sun's gone down. The enthusiasm to which I refer is, of course, the competition car brand that takes him all over Britain to speak wherever car enthusiasts are gathered. With the proviso that the Marshall high point of the day comes when it is almost over, I decided to keep tabs on Gerry for a couple of days and join him for one of the many DTV-Castrol forums that have been part of his way of life for many years now.

So it was that, shortly after his son Gregor (after Gregor Grant the late Editor of *Autosport*) had been christened, I found myself outside a neat white and black suburban property in Garston. The house itself just looks whiter and better maintained than its neighbours, but the driveway crescent of concrete holds both his white 3-litre engined BMW 525 automatic (since replaced by a Rover 3500) and his second (and they had only just been announced, literally days previously) Chevette HS2300. That car is registered 4 DTV , so providing a plate that does not exactly tax his famous human computer number plate recall. An ordinary looking front to the spacious garage alongside the house actually hides away a beautiful 1936 Armstrong Siddeley, the well kept secret of the mint 10,000 mile 1959 3.4 Jaguar, it may contain his beautiful Lister-Jaguar, plus the resident pair of thundering performance motorcycles: a BMW R100S Motorsport and one of the last Norton 850 Commandos. Elsewhere in the country there are yet more cars, but in proper wheeler-dealer tradition it's difficult to establish who owns what at any particular time. Suffice it to say that Marshall's taste in classic sporting machinery is to the kind of exacting level you would expect from a man of his background and interests.

Gadgets fascinate Gerry to this day. He has many wristwatches, there's the car telephone (a vital gadget in this case) and we spent nearly twenty minutes re-running video recordings. One of them the 1977 Thruxton TV saloon car race when poor Jock Robertson eventually spun and heavily damaged his Opel GS/E while fighting for the lead at the chicane. I say poor Jock, as Marshall naturally takes constant delight in re-running the split second of lost adhesion!

It is about ten in the morning when I call and the house is buzzing, the quietest member being young Gregor, who proves charmingly non-Marshall in his behaviour, gurgling quietly in the corner of his father's trophy room. Of course there is a bar in the room as well, but the sheer weight of silverware above constantly threatens to meet the tide of photos below and engulf would-be inebriates in past glories.

There is a lady busily 'doing for' the Marshalls in another corner of the room, while the kitchen is graced by Mrs. Carol Marshall. As usual she is trying gently to prod Gerry into arriving somewhere within the right day for his next appointment. To put it mildly, Gerry has a generous sense of time, his only real interest in the subject appearing on the *139* track, or when an unwise barman feels it's "time gentlemen please".

The house is as spick and span within as outside, but very much along average middle class lines with absolutely no signs of flashiness in any way. Gerry himself is also wary of flashy-looking cars the then current BMW being well-equipped and carrying another personal plate (NHW 4) but nothing that would attract any but the really knowledgeable bystanders' attention.

When Gerry is going into the business he's likely to set off at a great rate of knots, just before eleven o'clock and arrive around the chiming of that hour, the car ticking gratefully into coolness outside the Temple Fortune showroom's plate glass windows! On the day I joined him he had the pleasure of a brief visit from Bette Hill, Graham Hill's widow, warning Gerry of the consequences of his book pinching any sales from hers, Marshall returning the good natured teasing by asking her to identify the bare bottoms displayed in an old BRSCC annual dinner dance picture ... as you'd expect of a Lady, she got them wrong!

Marshall was especially busy around the time this book was written because, after a decade of running primarily with someone else's car, he was getting his own machinery together. This meant that he was frequently to be glimpsed setting new UK Allcomer's records for freestyle motorway endurance and speed, gathering together parts for his Triumph Dolomite Sprint, which then lived in Coventry. The deal in which he raced the Triplex Capri for the year was characteristic too: he and the previous recipient of the sponsorship, Colin Vandervell, met the Triplex PR man to sign the deal up on a London railway station. Neither of the drivers had met the man before, but it all went off smoothly and the Triplex representative (ex-Leyland PR man Mike Beard) got straight back on the next train to the Midlands with the agreement successfully signed. I still don't know who was most surprised!

We have already summarised the story of the Marshall Wingfield showroom but one can only reiterate that it is a place to visit, with its showroom always full of the unexpected. On one occasion Gerry had the famous *Old Nail* Firenza club racer and his Spa Twenty Four Hour Magnum on the premises, and there's nearly always something of competition interest in stock. With the capable David 'Lord' Atkinson on one side, the delectable Fiona on the other, the atmosphere is friendly but definitely businesslike. There are funny stories to be recounted by passing strangers about things that have gone wrong - one young assistant crushing a customer's 'droop snoot' Firenza up against the roof with an hydraulic lift when trying to goad some pre-delivery work along! Such disasters are exceptional though, for Gerry tends to keep a very sharp eye out for details that could go wrong.

Lunch time is truly impossible to summarise. On a bad day for writers a session at the Victoria, followed by the menace of afternoon drinking at the Little House Club, not far from the Steering Wheel Club in London's West End, can leave the onlooker with nothing but a painful head. Usually the collaborator in such deadly sessions is Tony Lanfranchi, the stories growing even more outrageous as time slips by and interlopers slide under the table/bar, or even out of the window!

It's equally possible that Gerry will stay in his showroom and work, or merely join fellow local trader Alan Foster over a pint or three and a sandwich at a nearby pub. Foster will be teased about his gentlemanly reference to skidding (he was actually a very successful MG factory driver for Dick Jacobs) and the two will probably swop some cars, or deal in some way during the break.

The afternoon could well be just a normal routine affair, but during our time together Gerry was pretty involved with fighting a legal battle with the RAC over a production saloon car ruling. His memory for facts and figures, plus the determination not to be outdone, will often result in such disputes, though it is obviously rare for them to go quite so far, quite so expensively, as the Opel case did in 1978. Another likely alternative to routine business is that he will be out doing something for publicity, and it

Three-wheeling the Magnum toward the finish of the Spa 24 Hours in Belgium. Peter Brock and I finished second overall, and Vauxhall won the team prize. *Courtesy Colin Taylor.*

was that trait which made him so important to Vauxhall as they struggled to establish a sporting name. They could not have chosen a more 'visible' driver, both in the obvious sense and in the way in which he works to ensure that what he is doing, and what he is doing it with, is widely known. A good example was that he was chosen to conduct an Escort 1300 rally car as one of the guest celebrity drivers for *Cars and Car Conversions* in 1978, so one day was spent at a photo studio with a Ford and the other pilots - people like Barry Lee and Andy Dawson. In similar vein there are the columns he writes (in the early days he did reports of his own sprint meetings, and did them just as well as the professionals, if the finished result is anything to go by) and there have been a couple of films too, including the one we are to see as part of tonight's forum: *There's Only One Gerry*. This is a Barry Hinchcliffe/United Motion Pictures production covering the very successful 1976 season.

Tonight's forum is at Vauxhall dealership in Bishops Stortford. That's within an hour's motoring of DTV's Shepreth home and, unusually, Billy Blydenstein is amongst the audience, tucked away at the back. His presence doesn't moderate the strength of Gerry's comments later that evening!

While several hundred shuffle to their seating we await the appearance of Marshall to join fellow panel member Chrissie Ashford (very definitely female), the Vauxhall engineer who handles DTV liaison (Roy Cook) and Roger Willis of Castrol: the latter doesn't really need a title. Like Marshall he's an institution and it would be no exaggeration to say that to most enthusiasts Roger Willis *is* Castrol.

Tonight we are sheltered in a small VIP room prior to the forum, sharing with a barrel of Green Abbott ale that has little idea of the threat posed to its existence by the occupant of a flying Chevette HS2300 even now homing in on the premises. DTV Roadshow co-ordinator John Foden and Willis are twitching over their watches, as Marshall howls through the night muttering "who is Pentti Airikkala anyway? Finn ...

Schminn!"

The Hinchliffe film is going down well outside. It reminds me how often Marshall has carried a camera in his cars, even when in the thick of competition. The point is brilliantly made in the last Brands Hatch round of the 1976 RAC Touring Car Championship, when Marshall not only has pole position with his Magnum 2300 in the damp practice, but also deadly class rival Andy Rouse (Broadspeed Dolomite Sprint) and the Capri horde to fend off. The camera stays in the car and, for anyone who has competed a little, the result is electrifying as you will Marshall to hold on to the lead gained by his customarily brilliant start.

You can feel the beads of anxious sweat around his neck and forehead as he cranes into the mirror, well aware that the dry conditions will bring the Capris a chance to exploit their extra speed on the straights. For nearly a complete lap of the GP circuit he stays in front, his gearchanges (through the five-speed ZF) are beautifully swift and positive, and there is also an apparent lack of his normal sideways style. Gordon Spice's Capri does charge by as they exit Clearways, but Marshall does manage to defeat the Dolomite, which was all that was required that October day.

The sequence around Mallory Park of him driving *Baby Bertha* is quite terrifying from inside as it is being warmed up on cold slicks: this leads to the kind of steering jerkiness that would do credit to a Keystone Cops movie. That ultimate Superloon is obviously very quick in a straight line, a feeling doubly emphasised by Mallory's claustrophobic length. The shots showing the amount of sheer opposite-lock he applies to come out of the hairpin underlines the torque of that bellowing 5-litre V8, which is soon comparatively quiet as the car settles into Devils Elbow.

Highlight of the film for laughter is a chance remark from Tony Strawson, edited into family viewing form, this fellow Superloon competitor replying pungently to the query "Why is that Vauxhall so quick?" Strawson quips : "It's got the biggest driver!"

The panel for the forum emerges comparatively unscathed by the barrel of Green Abbott, only slightly delayed by the effervescent Marshall's arrival and consequent need for refreshment: he's staying at a local hotel tonight. Gerry hopes that it is not like previous accommodation where, "they shut the bar early - in September!"

The rows of portable chairs are surrounded by posters propagating the link between General Motors and James Hunt, DTV and Castrol, plus the availability of Sportparts to make your Vauxhall into a car fit for heroes to dwell within. The audience is obviously composed of hard core enthusiasts, but the striking thing is that no particular age group predominates, and there's a fair sprinkling of women taking an interest too.

From Gerry's reactions and some experience, the people of Bishops Stortford have much the same questions to ask as anywhere else in the country. To get things rolling he's asked what he is going to do now that the Vauxhall racing contact has terminated? Characteristically, Blydenstein's presence or no, Gerry's razor-like dismantling of any PR pretensions begins. "There was talk of a rallycross car, because I'd been a good lad. I've been getting terribly drunk in the bar thinking what fun it would have been, but it's all gone quiet.

"I'm going to drive something made in Dagenham... called Crapi. Oh, *Capri*, sorry Stuart [touches imaginary forelock in deference to Ford's Stuart Turner]. I want to drive a 3-litre car like everyone else.

"I'm also supposed to be doing some development work on Chevette - but I expect I'll mow the lawn, beat the wife (Carol smiles almost wistfully, partially hidden amongst the audience) and even play with the kids.

"They kindly gave me the old Firenza, saves putting us both out to grass I suppose, and I ran that at Brands last week [he did *not* say that he set overall fastest time] rather than polish it up for a museum".

As he said that he is looking for sponsorship the audience are quick to suggest Ind Coope, but Gerry is quick to dismiss this as impractical: "I'm a Watney's man (Mann?)".

It's Formula Ford with a roof on top! The ex-Vandervell Capri and I seen at Brands Hatch during my 1978 season with the Ford in the national British series. *Courtesy Colin Taylor.*

Even the technical questions are directed at Gerry, the panel chairman having to make a conscious effort to steer questions to anyone but Marshall throughout the evening. Marshall is sincerely complimentary about the Chevette in all its forms, recommending that the 1500 Blydenstein conversion is kept for enthusiasts while he has also been trying to : "talk the wife into a 1256 Chevette: this is a super little car. You can drive it flat out and not have an accident!"

Marshall then goes on to talk about the potent 2.3-litre, 16-valve Chevette HS2300 he has just acquired (he sold the first straight after a class win at the Brands sprint!) and he says: "I'm going to make this one into a real roadburner. There's no point in just 110-115 mph. It's got to be 135 mph and that'll really frighten me: that's good value". A chortle comes over the PA, and his hands start to rub together with anticipatory glee as the rally questions start coming in. Among the rejoinders are those below.

"I think there are more characters in rallying, people like Evans, Churchill and (of course) Roger Albert Clark. Now he was the kingpin when I had the Ford drive and people reckoned he was a bit stand-offish. I got on with him alright, but I think that was because I didn't know when he was being rude!

"Then there's Pentti [Airikkala, Vauxhall's Finnish superstar]: he'll be OK... when he's joined the first division of drinkers.

"I have always said, when I get old and slow, I'll go rallying, or you don't have to be quick to be a rally driver, just dangerous. It's obvious that, if you can't find anything better to do on a Saturday night than sit beside some sweaty fella, then you deserve to be a rally driver!

"It always seems such a shame to me. Billy B puts lovely shiny cars together and these great oafs come along and smash them into a million pieces. We made racing cars last for three or four years. If a rally driver gets a car to last two events, he's doing well!"

The other half of the story in '78 was this Championship-leading Dolomite Sprint. It even won some races outright and you can see it here showing Lanfranchi (Opel) a textbook approach to cornering line! *Courtesy Colin Taylor.*

Inevitably this draws Roger Willis to some defence of the rallyist. He feels Marshall only goes racing because : "Its the only branch of the sport where he can find his way back to the start". After Gerry has recounted his best ever accident, with a DTV car on the Manx rally ("...actually you weren't even in the event!" Willis comments) the Castrol man also recounts his version of why Gerry had the accident at all. "The navigator shouted ninety degrees left: Marshall looked at the speedometer and saw it only read 75mph, so he speeded up until they had the accident!"

The inevitable debate over whether racing or rally drivers are the better breed draws an interesting reminiscence from Gerry: "We were out on a thing called the Catseyes Rally in 1900 and frozen to death. It was very foggy. Suddenly we were overtaken by a Morris Minor! The navigator was sitting head down and wittering inside this granny's car. I later discovered who this pair of right hooligans were; Pat Moss and Stuart Turner".

There is no doubt about it, the other members on the panel might just as well have stayed at home, save the girl who exploits her sex cleverly in some driver-navigator jokes. Gerry Marshall really is Vauxhall after all these years, and his assembled public is obviously as puzzled as he was to be dropped from the active competitive side.

It would be overstating the case to say that Vauxhall have made a terrible error, though. Their expensive rally programme has brought them the chance of standing up to, and beating Ford, under a blaze of publicity that just would not be realised in British national racing. It was having Marshall at all that brought Vauxhall to the point of credibility where they could embark on such international competition, but nobody has ever said that such a stalwart pioneering role would be rewarded. Not quite a prophet without honour, more of a saviour without the means to carry on preaching actively.

As Gerry's father commented to me: "Gerry's always been the centre of attention". And to prove that still applies, Gerry was doing better than ever this year when this was written. He had already clinched the ShellSport Derwent Production Saloon Car Championship and was poised to win the similar Britax Championship in the Triumph Dolomite Sprint. Out of twenty-three starts in the Dolomite Gerry had amassed an astonishing twenty-one class wins, including three outright victories, and two seconds. With or without Vauxhall, there's no doubt that Gerry Marshall will continue as the name no-one can ignore in British motor racing programmes.

Appendix: Marshall's Vauxhall career

February 28 1967: Competition debut of 1159cc Viva HB, sponsored by Shaw & Kilburn and driven by W.B. Blydenstein in CUAC Snetterton Sprint. Class win.

November 19 1967: Marshall's first race drive in 1258cc Shaw & Kilburn Special Viva. Finishes 8th overall. Viva competed in sprints and club races in the hands of either W.B. Blydenstein, Han Akersloot or Gerry Marshall.

June 9 1968: Debut of 2-litre Vauxhall Viva GT, still sponsored by Shaw & Kilburn. Driven by Gerry Marshall to 8th overall, 3rd in class. Best lap time at this meeting in the Brands Hatch Club Circuit was 62.4s. The Vauxhall offers approximately 125bhp in carburated form.

July 14 1968: Brands Hatch mini-circuit, Marshall finishes 2nd overall.

July 20 1968: Marshall takes first outright win for non-V8 engined Viva and for a Blydenstein Vauxhall. In twelve laps of Lydden Hill track he records a best lap of 52.6s (66.91mph).

December 27 1968: Viva appears for first time with Tecalemit-Jackson fuel injection, system retained for all Blydenstein four-cylinder race engines, giving 160bhp at debut.

In 1968 Viva scores 2 outright wins; 3 seconds, a fourth overall and two class wins with three other class positions recorded in twenty outings covering races, sprints, and hillclimbs. Blydenstein (races) and (once) Tony Lanfranchi share driving, Marshall all other races.

April 4 1969: Marshall wins Viva's first televised race at Oulton Park, by 0.4s!

May 1969: New 2310cc Viva club racer announced for Marshall at Shepreth launch. Engine has 97mm bore and 77mm stroke and claimed 200 (nett) bhp.

June 7 1969:   New car runs at Oulton, but on 2-litre engine. DNF, throttle jammed.

July 27 1969:   Viva 2.3 races at Snetterton. Breaks halfshaft after lapping in 48.2s.

August 9 1969:   Marshall contributes 25 laps to Viva Team's winning performance in Holland Birkett six hour relay, Silverstone Club Circuit.

August 30 1969:   Marshall takes 2.3's first win at Oulton Park. Marshall sole Shaw & Kilburn Viva driver this season. Scores 4 outright wins, 7 seconds and 2 third places from 21 Vauxhall race starts. Finished 2nd to George Whitehead (1860 Anglia) in Redex Saloon Car Championship.

March 1970:   2-litre International Group 2 Viva in Shaw & Kilburn colours makes racing debut at Brands Hatch Race of Champions supporting event for Vauxhall's first appearance in RAC British National Championship. Car DNF after accident at Dingle Dell.

Viva with 170bhp is no match for newly homologated BDA-Cosworth equipped Ford Escort and becomes un-reliable trying to keep up. Best result in year is a third in class at Thruxton: two DNFs owing to accidents. However, club car continues with now more reliable production crankshaft to give 2.3 litres. Marshall wins 5 races outright, scores one 2nd place and 3 third overalls, plus a win in the unlimited capacity class of the BARC Osram Championship, 1970.

Marshall finishes 16 races and three sprints with 2-litre Vivas, takes two FTDs and a class win in the sprints.

May 16 1970:   Viva makes its overseas debut with Marshall driving at Spa-Francorchamp saloon car races. Practices 2nd fastest to Ickx in wet, finishes 4th in dry race. Later in the year Viva also appears at Zolder, Belgium, and also finishes 4th overall.

May 29 1971:   Debut of 2.6-litre Viva engine, Marshall wins at Thruxton. New engine torque is rated at 210lb.ft & "over 200bhp" and during the season 2.2, 2.3, 2.5 and 2.6-litres versions of Vauxhall's SOHC four have raced. Favourite is 2.5-litre combination.

June 1971:   Dealer Team Vauxhall formed, cars change livery and lose Shaw & Kilburn orange and white for subsequent DTV, Thames TV, or DTV-Castrol liveries.

148 **September 9 1971:**   2.5-litre Vauxhall Firenza presented officially to

Thames TV and Eamon Andrews by Alan Maidens, DTV Chairman.

September 16 1971: Thames TV Firenza practices at Crystal Palace, but Gerry races Viva.

September 26 1971: Firenza makes race debut at Llandow, S. Wales. Wins 2 races and sets new record in Marshall's hands.

November 20 1971: Firenza wins for Marshall on TV from Lydden Hill, but Roger Bell and Mike Crabtree crash the Vivas, which are not used again by DTV. Using the Vivas and Firenza Marshall secures big class Championship in Osram series with 8 wins in 12 races, a pair of 2nd places and 5 lap records.

Altogether Marshall has contested 23 races for Vauxhall and won 18 of them. He is fifth overall in the *Autosport* annual 'league' of club race winners (22 wins in all, the others in his Championship - winning Escort Mexico; 24 victories in all that year including one in Vauxhall SOHC-engined Costin Amigo).

At the close of the year Marshall holds three lap records: Cadwell Park's 2.25 miles at 1m. 42.0s (79.41 mph), Llandow's 1 mile at 39.2s (91.84mph) and Lydden's 1 mile track at 47s (76.60mph).

March 1972: Opening round of the two Group 1 Championships operated that year. Vauxhall contest Castrol series, first with DTV Firenza 2000 and subsequently with Firenza 2300 homologated during course of year.

Marshall has an eventful year with two accidents, plus loss of rear wheel twice at Brands Hatch, and points removal on engine size scrutineering. Scores two 2nd places overall, 7 class wins and 4 class seconds. Wins class in Castrol series.

October 1972: Marshall declared Forward Trust outright saloon car champion with a race to go in 2.5 Thames TV Firenza carrying Esso decals. In 13 rounds of series he wins 9, is 2nd twice and 3rd once. During the year he has 15 wins in the Firenza and finishes 4th in the *Autosport* league, having also driven other cars for a final tally of 20 outright victories, plus 7 class wins, and holder of two lap records during year.

Marshall awarded BARC President's Cup.

March 11 1973: Firenza's race debut with 2.2 (later 2.3)-litre version of the Lotus LV 240 engine with DOHC and 16-valves. Despite practice and pre-practice troubles Marshall *149* wins, averaging 89.28mph (fastest lap: 52.8s/92.84mph). During the year dry sump lubrication and a five-speed gearbox (for the first time on a competition Vauxhall) improves reliability, DTV claiming 21 outright victories with the car and securing a class championship title in the Forward Trust series.

A single outing in the Group 1 Firenza brought him to 22 outright Vauxhall wins that year, and there was a class win (3rd overall) in Viva 1800 which brought him fourth place in the annual *Autosport* Club Race Winners tables.

October 3 1973: Hilton Hotel, London is the scene for Vauxhall announcement of DTV Ventora V8, the car later dubbed *Big Bertha*. Car does not race that year, but is shown at Motor Show Earls Court with its 480bhp 5-litre Repco Holden V8 engine and Vauxhall-styled coach-work. Also in October, Firenza 2.3 club racer is timed at 133mph at Silverstone, where it first appears with the 5-speed gearbox.

January 1974: BRSCC announce new 'Superloon' eight-race Championship, £1250 prize fund.

March 31 1974: Ventora's debut with Marshall on Silverstone Club Circuit. Wins from pole position with a fastest lap of 58.2 (99.46mph). Marshall's 1st outright win at Silverstone.

June 27 1974: Marshall's 50th Vauxhall Firenza win.

August 4 1974: Ventora written-off officially following Silverstone accident after brake pads dropped out. Car raced six times and won on three occasions, taking the Silverstone lap record. Firenza provided 14 wins, 9 seconds and 1 third during the year, plus a new lap record at Oulton Park. With the help of both cars Gerry Marshall became 1974 Forward Trust Saloon Car Champion outright. Marshall takes 17 outright wins for Vauxhall and sixth place in Club Race Winners when a single class win (Avenger) is included.

March 5 1975: Launch of Chevette. Funeral of Hank Clark, Vauxhall sales director and one of the driving forces behind DTV ... DTV had also assumed reponsibility for the ex-Coburn rallying programme with Magnum.

May 5 1975: Last outing in Firenza at Silverstone Club layout. Marshall achieved his ambition by lapping in 60s for a lap in the car, which finished fourth overall and had won 63 races. Car presented to Marshall 1978.

May 22 1975: Tested *Baby Bertha* the Firenza with Ventora's 5-litre engine and other parts installed by DTV at Shepreth: under existing Snetterton record with Marshall at wheel in first runs.

May 25 1975:

Firenza V8 race debut at Brands Hatch Ford Sport Day. Laps in 50.3s but retires after 3 laps when 3rd overall (driveshaft failure).

June 2 1975:

Mondello Park, Ireland, wins two races in Firenza V8, first of many!

July 19 1975:

Firenza V8 wins Superloon supporting race to British GP by 38s, averaging 110.10mph and recording fastest lap of 1m 35.0s.

Firenza V8 wins 18 of 20 races started, Marshall wins 1975 Tricentrol Super Saloon Car Championship and holds lap records at (amongst others): Brands Hatch Club Circuit 49.2s (90.73mph) and Silverstone GP (1m 33.8s); Silverstone Club, (57.0s); Thruxton (1m 22s) and Mallory Park (47.2s).

November 1975:

Marshall completes Group 1 production Saloon Car Championship; programme that commenced in March. Driving Hamilton Motors Magnum 2300 he contests 30 races, but misses rounds of series with other commitments, scores six class wins.

March 14 1976:

Brands Hatch, Marshall returns to a season of contesting the RAC British Saloon Car Championship with 190bhp Group 1 Magnum, new car supplied by DTV after opening round in which Marshall takes a class win, 4th overall. Subsequently wins class three times (including one 2nd overall at Brands Hatch in closing round) and takes class Championship.

March 2 1976:

Marshall contests first of 17 from 20 rounds that he is able to tackle in Radio 1 Championship with Hamilton Motors Magnum 2300. Goes on to take class championship with 13 class wins, two 2nds and a 3rd.

May 8 1976:

Firenza V8 is beaten for only time during year (J. Buncombe's *Chimp* which was barred thereafter) at Silverstone. Firenza and Marshall take Tricentrol Super Saloon Car Championship title for 2nd year running. During the year the V8 takes 9 wins from 11 starts and 1 second place.

December 31 1976:

Firenza V8 and Marshall holds records at: Brands Hatch Club, 48s, (90.37mph); Castle Combe, 1m 3.0s (105.14mph); Mallory Park 47.2s (102.97mph); Silverstone GP 1m 33.33s (113.10mph); Snetterton, 1m 8.2s (101.19mph) and Thruxton, 1m 20.4s (105.49mph).

March 1977: First appearance of the year in RAC Group 1 series. Suffered puncture and broke lap record four times, leaving it at 1m 47.11s (98.55mph). At the end of year no class wins, but held class record at Brands Hatch in the 1976 Magnum 2300 at 1m 45.58s (89.12mph).

July 22/23 1977: Gerry Marshall/Peter Brock (Group 1 Magnum 2300) take Vauxhall's best overseas result since DTV was formed, 2nd overall in Spa-Francorchamps 24 Hours race: Vauxhall also win *Coupe du Roi* team prize. Their Magnum covers 2412.55 miles at 100.52mph average, winning class *en route*.

October 27 1977: DTV announce that their plans for 1978 do not include racing but that: "Gerry Marshall will remain with DTV in a consulting capacity".

October 30 1977: In a race for Special Saloons over 8 laps of the Thruxton circuit Marshall and *Baby Bertha* Firenza V8 make their last appearance for DTV. They win at a 96.08mph average: it is only the Firenza V8's second appearance of the year in Britain, and only its third in the year (the car visiting Denmark) - naturally Marshall and his Firenza V8 also won that other event, at Donington.

November 1977: Marshall completes his Hamilton Motors Magnum 2300 Group 1 schedule. The Vauxhall has taken 7 class wins and retires having won 27 class victories, including one race outright on the Silverstone GP circuit (1976, for the Marshall Wingfield Trophy in the wet!), no mean feat against 3-litre opposition. The Hamiliton Motors Magnum, maintained by John Bott, held five class lap records at the end of 1977: Brands Hatch GP, 1m. 58.4s (78.47mph); Mallory Park, 59.6s (81.54mph); Oulton Park, 1m. 19.6s (74.80mph); Silverstone GP, 2m. 3.1s (85.74mph) and Snetterton, 1m. 25.4s (80.81mph).

Index

Index

Acknowledgements

My sincere thanks for their help in the compilation of this book go to those mentioned below. Special thanks must go to the Marshall family for their help at such a sad time during the preparation of this tribute edition. Unsung heroes must include some of the photographers whose work could not be credited. To them, and all those who are mentioned, my thanks.

Clive Richardson
Mike Kettlewell
Linda McRae
W. B. Blydenstein
Paul Davies
Colin Taylor Productions
Roy Cook
Simon Taylor
Terry Grimwood
Roger Bell
Anthony Curtis
Jeff Bloxham
John Gaisford
Motoring News
Motor Sport
Autosport
Hot Car
Colin Wood
John Davenport
John Horton
Gerry Johnstone
Dick Waldock
David Atkinson
Albert Marshall
Carol Marshall
Gregor Marshall
Gary Hawkins
LAT Photographic
Ted Walker

Finally, thanks to Gerry Marshall, who supplied the entertaining bits.

Jeremy Walton